About t

Norma Ellis was raised on one of the highest mountain tops in Jamaica. Born in the fifties, at the age of five her father had travelled to England and within the first three months of his departure both her grandmother passed away and Norma was diagnosed with a hole in her heart. In order to survive, she had to leave her mountain top home to begin a long journey without her parents or siblings to fight for her life.

She was not expected to live past the age of ten, but her story of survival faced many challenges of learning to take care of herself, in the wake of the death of her friends who had not survived their own heart illness. Fate was on her side and her life saving journey bought her to England were she was one of the first five children who pioneered the first experiments for a heart valve replacement.

Norma was the only child to survive the experiment and went on to achieve other pioneering challenges during the racism of the seventies. She opened doors for black women to work in an office environment, retail and in the beauty industry, Norma was the first black beauty consultant in Birmingham. After setting beauty trends working on the first black beauty and hair magazine, black Beauty exhibitions, television as a make-up artist and teaching black women a new lifestyle in the world of beauty and cosmetics. Norma gave up her successful career in beauty to travel to Europe and work in the sex industry.

After many years she reinvented herself back into the beauty industry and experienced a whole new life in the United States of America but found herself back in England, the country that saved her life. A story about the survival of fighting to live, sex, fall in love, fighting racism while pioneering changes to the black Beauty industry that recently had a market value of millions. Norma is now a Beauty Assessor and a Transformational Podcaster.

To Dick

Norma's autobiographical account is raunchy! Fasten your seatbelt! Sit tight!

Coming down from my mountain top

Norma Ellis

You are about to embark on a journey to Erotica!

From Phyllis, a friend of Norma! Enjoy the Ride!

Dedication

This book is dedicated to my wonderful son Justin, my beautiful granddaughter Kaya.

And to my incredible mom and dad for having the courage to take the opportunity they were given to save my life. May they continue to rest in perfect peace. To my Chocolate Boy when you showed up I found my true self.

Review Request

Dear reader, I greatly appreciate your purchasing my book, and I hope you enjoy it as much as I enjoyed writing it.

Once you finish reading the book, if you don't mind, I would love to get your feedback.

Please leave a review at amazon.com & amazon.co.uk

Contents

Introduction

Everyone has his or her own journey, and though the result is the same, the road travelled to get there differs.

If you sometimes feel abandoned, remember that we have never been abandoned. We are never alone as God the universe is always with us.

My dearest mother, no one knows what the future holds, but we dream and wish.

From the age of five, my future did not look bright, but your dreams, wishes, and prayers came true. I know because I was not expected to live, but I made it to sixty-two years. That's when I wrote this to you.

Your strength and courage shone through some very challenging and difficult times. As a mother, you never gave up, and I learned from you never to give up either.

My dearest father, your love remains strong in my heart with every beat it takes.

Chapter 1
The Early Years

I was born into a family of love on one of the highest mountaintops in the West Indies. My mother and father were neighbours as children, so they knew each other growing up. My parents were very influential in our community. My father's family was big; he had many brothers and sisters, and most of the people in the community were related in some way or another. My mother knew she wanted to marry my father from a very young age. When she was fifteen years old, she sent him an anonymous letter asking him to meet her somewhere in the city. My father turned up on what you could say was a blind date. She kept my father waiting before she finally put in her appearance, hiding and observing him to see how he was handling the blind date. Just as my father was ready to give up and leave, she finally appeared. He was pleasantly surprised to see her.

They were both beautiful people. My father was very handsome, and all the women in our community were crazy for him. My mother was a beauty to behold. While my father was quiet and strong, my mother was fiery, bold, and strong.

My father was twenty-three years old at the time of their blind date, eight years older than my mother. He was already established as a good provider. He left school at the age of thirteen and was a trained builder who also owned a farm. My father was a very disciplined man, and although he was the catch of the community, he never had children with anyone other than my mother. My father enjoyed life and focused on being successful. He had a big heart for people and his community; he loved his brothers and sisters dearly and was supportive of his family. They all looked up to him for guidance and counted on him to keep the peace.

My mother was from a much smaller family and only met her father once, when he gave her a farthing. She was the eldest of her known siblings, but it's likely she has other siblings too. Her mother had a son with another man but married the father of her other two daughters. My mother grew up with her grandmother, who lived until she was over one hundred years old.

At the time, we should have paid more attention to our great-grandmother and asked her to share her stories, as she was a child at the time slavery ended.

My parents started their life together in a good position and would have been considered well-off in those days. My father built his own house and by then owned two farms. They were a great team. My mother was fiery and "wore the trousers" in the family. My father was cool, calm, and strong. He was the only person who could put my mother's fire out. She loved him passionately.

Very soon, they started a family and had two boys. By this time, my father's life had changed; he had become a born-again Christian. It took some time before my mother converted as she enjoyed going to dance halls. One night, my father told her that he would lock the door and not let her back in their home if she went out. She gave up and soon became a born-again Christian. They got married and became active members of the community church, which was next to our house. My father's faith and his beliefs were strong, and he became a preacher for the church. My mother became a Sunday school teacher for young children and carried the title of *Mother to the Community* until the day she died.

With a strong commitment to each other, my parents went on to have four more children—my eldest sister, me, a younger sister, and a younger brother. My early memories are from when I was around three years of age. Most of them are vague, but some are strong though I can't recall how far apart they occurred. When you are young, everything seems like a lifetime, and it's difficult to understand how to measure time. One of the stories my mother loved to tell was about my father leaving for England when I was only two weeks old. He stayed in England for two and a half years. He missed my mother and his children so much that he did not stay the entire time he had planned.

Some early memories of my parents and siblings were of my older sister and me fighting to sit on our father's knees while he was eating, so that we could eat from his plate. My sister would sit on one knee, and I would sit on the other. For some reason, the food on my father's plate tasted sweeter than what we ate from our own. He would feed us each tiny piece of cut-up food from his plate. My sister is three years older than I am, and she would not give him up. She would always tell me that he was her daddy first. Boy, we used to fight over our father for his attention.

I remember going to the community church school and playing with my cousin in the churchyard. We sat in the long, green grass, and the boys caught lizards with the grass blades. Slowly, they lowered the lizards down onto our backs as we sat talking about childish things. The lizards would stick to our backs as we jumped and screamed, trying to shake them off.

Our house was on a large plot of land with many fruit trees. We also grew coffee. I remember two occasions when my father was not pleased with me. My sister had forgotten her schoolbooks, and since there was no one at home, she pushed me up to climb through a window to get them. I don't know how my father knew, but you could not do anything without your parents knowing about it in those days.

The other time he was not pleased with me was when I wanted to use the toilet, but there was a lizard sitting on the toilet seat. I was afraid of lizards because of the nasty little boys putting them down my back. I threw stones at the lizard on the toilet, but it just kept moving from side to side. When I finally managed to hit it, I said, "You behind, got you!" My father overheard me, and to him, *behind* was a bad word. He asked me what I had said. "I don't know, sir," I told him (we had to address him as "Sir"). "Daddy," I told him, "I said 'your beice', Sir."

Another vivid memory I have occurred at a big wedding with lots of people, cake, food, and dancing. I loved the music and dancing. I have vivid memories of playing in my grandmother's yard with my sister and cousins and going to school and church. On Sunday afternoon, my sister and cousin went to Sunday school at another community church not far from our house. I was allowed to accompany them on a few occasions.

In the community square on a Sunday afternoon, one of my male cousins would make and sell ice cream. He also sold shaved ice with syrup over it. We called it suck-suck.

The dirt on our mountaintop was red and the crumbling earth on the embankment was soft red stone. We used to pick it up and eat it. The taste was sweet. It was a treat that we didn't have to make or buy; we just ate it every day. Everyone in the community ate this red dirt. When my aunt was pregnant, we had to gather lots of it for her to eat.

I spent most of my time playing at my paternal grandmother's house. I had a great fondness for her. She was a full Indian woman and very beautiful, with long black Indian hair. We called both our grandmothers by special names. My father's mother we called Meme, and our mother's mother, Mama. Mama was a strong-minded woman, as was her mother, our great-grandmother, whom I was also attached to. We called her Muma. She was a real cornerstone in our lives and a strong force behind our mother. Muma nurtured all of us with so much love. She lived past the age of one hundred. I loved when she came home from the market because she always brought some special sweets or a toy with her. Muma was such an unusual woman. She used to smoke tobacco and in those days, they never had paper to roll the tobacco in, so they used dried tobacco leaves to roll the tobacco in the same way a cigar is made. Muma used to put the lit end in her mouth when she was coming to the end of her rolled tobacco. She would also blow the smoke through her ears and nose. To hide her grey hair, she mixed Vaseline with black shoe polish. And she had a special smell about her that was comforting to me as a child.

Muma was not from our district so sometimes we visited her in the district where she lived, in a little house situated in a forest, surrounded by trees. It was very frightening after dark with the creatures and sounds of the night. It would have made a perfect setting for a horror movie; I was so afraid of the night time at her house. When my sister and I slept over, we clung to each other all night long. Thank God we did not go too often. Instead, Muma came to our house and spent long periods with us.

When I was four years old, my younger sister was born. I remember coming home from school to the cries of a newborn. This meant my position had changed. I was no longer the baby, and the focus was now on my younger sister.

A few weeks after my fifth birthday, our mother was already seven months pregnant again. She would give birth to my youngest brother a few months later. Father decided to try his luck again in England before my mother gave birth to my youngest brother. I know this as it was a story that my mother talked about over and over again. It's amazing, but as hard as I try, I can't remember my mother with a big belly or being pregnant with my younger sister or brother. But I remember the days they were born as I came home from school to the cries and smells of newborns.

When my father left on his second trip to England, he went with many other members of the community, including his brother, his sister and her husband, and my mother's only brother and his wife. My cousin came to live with us at our house, along with his big, beautiful white dog named Bruno.

That Sunday morning the local method of transport—a big truck that carried people and food down from our mountaintop to the city—was full of people from the community. But the truck was not going to the market. At the time, they never told me where we were going, but now I know it was to the airport. This was my first time going to the city, although we could see it clearly from our mountaintop. It was scary to see so many people and large buildings. There was lots of crying from the women in our community and other women at the airport. My father and the others waved as they departed for England. Then we all went up to a particular place on the building, where I saw some huge birds. I watched my father, the others from our community, and some other people go up some steps and into the belly of the big bird. After they all entered, its doors closed, the stairs were removed, and the big bird flew high into the sky and disappeared. I started to cry as I felt something was wrong. Sadness clearly shone on my mother's face and on the faces of my older brothers, my sister, my cousin, and the other families from our community. My heart sank. I just knew I would not see my father again, at least not for a long time. But I could not work out for how long as I was still a child. You could say I was still a baby and had no understanding of time. And in those days, parents did not tell younger children the truth of what was happening. Only older children were privileged to that information, and it was left to them to tell the younger ones if they felt like doing so. Telling us was a powerful thing for the older children; they could tell us whatever they wanted in a way to control our fears.

I cried on the way home from the airport. The truck made a stop to pick up two passengers. One was a man from our community. With him was a handsome young boy about two years older than me. His name was Luke, and he would be staying with this foster family in our community. Luke sat beside me in the truck. I was still crying and in the darkness of the truck, he found my hand and held it all the way home. When I think about it now, I imagine he was also feeling pain and sadness as he had left his family to be fostered. From that moment in the truck, Luke and I became inseparable. We enjoyed playing for hours in the churchyard. From our mountaintop, we had a panoramic view of our island and down upon the city that I now know as Kingston. We could see the airport and the shipping port. I would watch the big birds landing and taking off. Sometimes, a big bird would fly over my mountaintop. I ran after the big bird, calling out, "Big bird! Bring my daddy back!" until it disappeared. I could never run fast enough to catch the big bird. Luke eased the sadness of not having my father around.

After my mother gave birth to my younger brother and my father left for England, a chain of events occurred all in the space of three months. This timeline was verified by my eldest brother. After the birth of my youngest brother, Mama (my grandmother) died. Before that, she had taken to her bed unwell. One day I went to her house, where I saw that they had laid her out on the floor in the corner of the living room. As usual, no one told me what was happening. Lots of activities were going on in the yard.

Papa, my step-grandfather, was cutting a big log

and shaving it down. I didn't know then, but now I know he was making a coffin. I could not understand why Mama was lying on the floor and would not open her eyes. I tried to open them. Then I called her name, but nothing happened. She just lay there, not moving. I was perplexed, and no one was giving me an explanation.

Another strange thing they were doing was digging a big hole in the ground on one side of the property. There were a lot of men digging this big hole and drinking. When the big box and hole were finished, they put Mama into the box and marched to the church. All the people in the community came. There was singing, talking and lots of crying. Then they marched back to the property and put the box into the hole they had dug. I was not sure what to do as I did not know what was happening. But from my mother and close family's crying, I felt it was not a good thing. I don't remember crying, but after they all had left, I sat on top of the hole they had dug, now covered with dirt. Now I know it was a grave. I sat there, talking to Mama, asking her why she had let them put her down into the ground and when she was going to come out. Of course, I never got an answer. For days I went back to sit on her grave and talk to her, but to no avail; she never came out or spoke to me. And no one told me that this was death.

A month later, it happened all over again, this time to Meme. Now my emotions were troubled. I wondered why all the people I loved the most were being taken away from me and if it was because of something I had done. The night Meme died, my cousin and I were sleeping in the bed with her. In the morning, she would not wake up. I tried to open her eyes. I called her name. But just like Mama, she would not move. We shouted for the grown-ups to come. By this time, I knew what was going to happen. I am not sure who told me that Meme was dead, but I knew that death meant she was never coming back. And I was never told a nice story about my grandmothers going to a special place called heaven and that I would see them there one day.

After Meme's death, I went into a deep sadness. Life had changed. I became fearful. My heart was totally broken with my father's going away, followed by Mama's and Meme's deaths. I could not see the beauty of life anymore. I could not, as a child, make sense of all these events or why they had to happen. Everyone became serious. My mother became harsher with all of us. She was responsible for her two younger sisters, her brother's children, and my cousin, who lived with us. Only my one cousin lived with us in our home. Also, as she was responsible for my father's three farms, she employed men to work. My mother also helped to run the community's politics. This was in addition to caring for her six children.

My eldest brother had more responsibilities and had to do well at school. He and my eldest sister went to private school. My second-eldest brother and my cousin went to a good normal school. My second-eldest brother loved all the farming, including looking after the goats. He also cooked, combed our hair, gave us baths, and made sure we ate. My eldest brother helped my mother with her business matters, like registering births and deaths and performing any other official business. By the time he was twelve, he had become a born-again Christian. He loved to sing and had a great voice. He also loved to make things and had his heart set on becoming an engineer, building bridges and roads.

My mother was a firm disciplinarian. With so many to take care of, she was known in the district as someone who would discipline anyone's child! And no one challenged her as she ran things, had the best jobs and money, and the best house.

Our house had survived a few hurricanes. During one very bad hurricane, we sheltered families who had lost their homes.

One day, my eldest brother had to go to town on an errand for my mother. He missed the truck to get back home and had to walk all the way in pitch-darkness. When the night is dark in Jamaica, it's very dark. How he saw his way home, only God knows. My mother was doing her ironing by the window in the living room. I was sitting opposite, watching her. My other siblings were in bed, and my cousin's dog, Bruno, was lying on the veranda, on guard. My mother was so cross and upset because my brother had gotten home so late. Instead of being thankful that he had gotten home safely, she was very angry with him. My mother turned back to her ironing. She had just ironed the ribbon that she used to tie the curtain and was hanging it on the nail on the window when both she and I saw her mother's face press close to the window. This window faced a narrow banking which was the darkest part of the property. At night we never walked around that side of the house as it was too dark. My mother cried out her mother's name with fear. Bruno barked and ran around the house. Mother quickly pulled the curtain shut and put out the fire in the stove. She bundled all of us in one bed in the middle bedroom of the house. She was terrified.

I believe that was Mama, showing my mother that she was not pleased with her anger at my brother as he was her favourite grandchild. I can't remember ever hearing my mother talk about what happened that night.

Chapter 2

Coming Down From
My Mountain Top

The most dramatic and life-changing day for me was a Sunday. It was still early as there were no sounds of birds. No clouds floated by. There was a quietness within me; I felt as if the world had stopped inside me. I did not want to go to church that morning. I just was not feeling well, but it was not a feeling I could describe or explain. My second-eldest brother stayed with me. He did not like going to church, so he was happy to stay at home with me and do the cooking. Cooking was done on an open fire in our kitchen, which was detached from our house. I was sitting on the doorstep of the house facing the kitchen, watching my brother cooking. As I talked with him, my nose started to bleed, blood pouring out like a river. I pinched my nose, but then the blood began pouring out of my mouth. I called out to my brother, and he ran to the church to get my mother. When she arrived, she could not stop the bleeding. So she lifted me up, wrapped me in the skirt she was wearing, and ran with me to the community square, where the truck driver lived. She got him to drive us to the hospital in the town.

This was no ordinary nosebleed; some of the blood came out as big clots. When we arrived at the hospital they padded my nose with gauze as deep in as it could go, but the blood just started coming down the back of my throat and I was vomiting blood. My mother had taken me to a private hospital. In those days, the children's cot frames were made out of metal, so I felt as if I was being put into a cage.

They worked on me all through the night. They used ice packs on my forehead to cool my blood down and I had to lie still on my side. The bleeding slowed down the following morning.

My mother said she was going to talk to the doctors, but she did not return. The hospital was built in a circle, and the ward I was in looked across to the corridors of the hospital where people were coming and going. I stood up in the cot and looked at the people in the hospital corridors. I saw my mother quickly running and then walking quickly, making her way out of the hospital. I felt so lost, frightened, and alone. I started crying. I put my feet through the bars of the cot and held onto it, shaking it as hard as I could, crying for my mother. I cried all day. I would not eat or drink anything, so they put a needle in my arm with a drip. At some point in the evening, I fell asleep, exhausted.

The next morning, I woke up and took to the same position. I cried all day. By the next day, the bleeding had stopped completely. I can't remember if I ate anything, but my position was the same in the cot, shaking it as I continued crying and hiccupping. And still, my mother did not come back.

Later in the day, a white lady with white hair was walking around with some doctors, looking at some of the other children. She came over to me. With a loving smile and a soft, tender voice, she asked about my history. She was told my mother had brought me in two days before with bleeding from my nose and mouth. The lady was so loving that I stopped crying. She asked me if she could listen to my chest, and when I said yes she put a very cold silver disc on my chest. After she listened for a while, she got them to take an X-ray of my heart. It was discovered that I had a leaking heart valve, so she had me moved the next day to the general hospital. There she had other children with heart conditions whom she looked after; having us all together was easier for her. Dr Angus worked in Florida at a heart hospital and came to Jamaica once a week to do pro bono work. In her absence, she left us in the care of a senior registrar doctor, who carried out her instructions.

I didn't know how my mother was going to find me or if she was coming back. I felt as if I had done something wrong for her to leave me at the hospital. I was in a big ward with a section for babies and young children, and it was there that I met Antony, an Indian boy who also had a heart problem. We quickly became strong friends.

My mother did turn up. How much later I can't say, but it felt like forever. From then on I often had to spend both short and long spells in hospital, and whenever my mother came to visit me, it was always a Sunday. She would bring almost all the people from the community as it was a day out for them. They were always interested to see for themselves that I was alive, as a story had spread about how bad I was. According to the stories, I was always near to death. My visitors filled up the ward, standing around my cot and looking at me as if I were some strange animal in the zoo they were seeing for the first time. As a child, I had nothing to say to all those people. I was just embarrassed and tried to focus on my brothers and sister. My mom never brought my younger brother or sister to visit me. Before my visitors left, they would be singing, praying, and having church.

I never liked any of it as it never really allowed me to have any privacy with my mother, brothers, sister, or close family and friends. As a matter of fact, it made me feel afraid. If Antony was in hospital with me during those periods, we would just laugh after they left.

One of the things that I looked forward to while I was in hospital was my mother bringing me talcum powder. There was only one brand of talcum powder in Jamaica at the time. It was in a red tin with a pretty lady with a white face painted on it. She was wearing a beautiful big hat. The brand was called Mavis. I not only loved the smell, but also I started eating the powder. And it worked just like the red dirt we all ate on our mountaintop. I missed that red dirt greatly. My mother could not understand how the talcum powder would finish so quickly, and I would say to her, "It's only a small tin," which it was.

When I was sent home from hospital, they put me on bed rest as our mountaintop was so high that it affected my breathing and, eventually, always brought on massive nosebleeds. Someone from the community told my mother that she should feed me lots of watercress as this would eventually fill the hole in my heart.

My mother bought a wooden cot for me to sleep in. It was in her room, and I became a prisoner in that room, never going outside. She had my second-eldest brother bring me so much watercress to eat every day. I hated it. He almost filled my cot with watercress as if I were an animal being fed. I had to find a way to get rid of all that watercress as I could not eat it. So when no one was around, I sneaked out of my cot. My mother's bedroom had a door leading out to the side of the house where there was a gully. I threw the watercress down the gully. I drank plenty of marijuana tea to stop the pain; that was the best-tasting tea.

Then the community said that I had an evil spirit in me. One time my mother took me to what we call the obeah man, or witch doctor, to get rid of the evil spirit. The room was lit only with candlelight. He bathed me in a big tin basin with cologne water. In Jamaica it was called *kalanga* water. He used a dead pigeon, its warm blood still pouring from it, to wash me. The feathers and bone from this dead pigeon scratched my skin all over. He repeated some prayer and told my mother I had to wear a red vest to ward off the evil spirit. Of course, none of this healed my heart.

I just could not live on my mountaintop anymore. It was too high, and I kept getting nosebleeds. So my mother had to find a foster family for me to live with near the hospital. One of the men who worked for my mother on the farm lived with his wife, son, and daughter not far from the hospital. He had already taken in one of my male cousins to go to a school in the city and a young girl from our community who they said had an evil spirit in her. She also had to wear a red vest, and they thought that these spirits were from our community. When I think about it, she had mental health issues.

So I was sent down from my mountaintop to live with this family. Their house was on an estate, but in Jamaica we called it a *tenement yard*. They had two rooms, an outdoor kitchen, and a toilet. The house was the last house on the estate. It led from the high road and had one of the biggest yards that had a dried-up stream at the bottom. Across from the dried-up stream was the beautifully manicured lawn of a boys' school. Only white boys and some privileged black boys could go to that school. They played cricket, and I enjoyed watching them as I was on my own during the day. I tried going to school when I was there but only managed to do a few days.

The husband stayed on the farm during the week and came home on Friday night. The wife went to work during the day, but I don't know what job she did. It was school for everyone else. The next-door neighbour—who had young children and a baby— kept her eyes on me, but sometimes she had to go out, and then I was really on my own.

The yard was full of big ground lizards that I now know as iguanas. They were the grey ones. They did not move around the yard, instead, there was one spot where they all gathered. They dug a hole and all piled on top of each other to keep cool. I never went around that side of the house as I was afraid of them. When the boys at the school came out for their break, I would get as close as I could to the gully and watch them play.

My mother left money for me to buy lunch every day. I did not know anything about time, but when I was hungry, I walked to the main road that was filled with lots of traffic and other activity. I had to cross the road every weekday to get to the shop where I would buy a bottle of D&G pineapple soda and a fairy cake (now known as cupcake). One day after buying my soda and fairy cake, I waited to cross the road. I looked both ways a few times, and when I could not see any cars coming, I started to cross. Then from nowhere, a car sped up and came down on me, almost hitting me. I froze in fright in the middle of the road. l had no memory of it until I came round on the sidewalk with lots of people around me. I sat up, shaken. Someone kindly picked up my cake and soda. God only knows how the soda bottle did not break from the fall. I got up trembling and slowly walked back to the house, everything inside me shaking. I ate my fairy cake and drank my soda while sitting on the doorstep. I never told anyone about that accident; this is the first time I am talking about it.

My foster parents' son was about eleven or twelve years old and tall. He went to the big school. Their daughter was no more than two years older than me. There was a single bed and one double bed in the parents' room. My cousin slept on the single bed during the week. As the husband was not there, I slept with the mother. In the other room was a double bed and a dining room table. Their son, their daughter, and the other foster daughter slept in that room. On the weekends, when the husband came back, I still slept in the bed with the parents. But I could not cope with sleeping with them as when they had sex, it exerted my heart, thereby restricting my breathing. So I sometimes slept in the bed with the son, the daughter, and the young girl. The son always made sure I slept beside him.

The day came when I had to go back into hospital. They had built a beautiful children's ward, so besides Antony and me with heart conditions, two other girls, Rosie and Gilda, joined us. Rosie was Indian. She was thin and very feeble. Gilda was plump and strong. We occupied the back section of the ward, and the young babies were at the front, closer to the nurses' station.

As fate would have it, every time I had to stay in hospital, Antony, Gilda, and Rosie were there too. We were all bedridden, but Gilda and I, who were the strongest, came off our beds to fill used syringes with water for ourselves and for Antony and Rosie to have water fights. Sometimes Rosie and Gilda argued, and Gilda would jump off her bed to go and hit Rosie.

When I was well enough to leave hospital, I did not go back to the foster parents. I went to stay with my mother's uncle and his wife. They had a son and a daughter. My mother's younger sister was already there when I arrived.

My uncle had cows. He kept them in the front yard at night, and during the day, he would take them to his farm. His property was big. The front yard was big enough to hold all his cows and the house with two bedrooms and a dining room. There was a small cemetery at the back with lime trees, an orange tree and a bird pepper tree. The property had a lower level, where the kitchen was, and some fenced space where my uncle kept pigs. Then on an even lower level was the toilet. From that level you could walk through a small tract with plenty of trees and come to the most beautiful waterfall. That's where we went to collect water.

I tried going to school for a while. I have some memories of making friends there and buying coconut drops at playtime or on my way home from school. There was a boy in my class who took a shine to me. His name was Campbell.

On the way home from school, the kids would tease me, singing a song they made up: "Mrs Campbell, you're going home to cook Mr Campbell's dinner." I could not stand the boy.

One of the things big people would say to frighten us so we went straight home from school was that there was a black-heart man who took children away. The fear of this man always caused us to hurry home from school.

Of course, my schooldays never lasted long, and I stayed by myself with the dogs and pigs as company. My mother did not come often to see me as her younger sister looked after me, and she was comfortable with her uncle and his wife caring for us. But my mother sent my eldest sister with money and packages as, by this time, my eldest brother was at university in the United States. With all my moving about, I never saw my younger brother or sister after I came down from my mountaintop.

During the period of staying with my uncle, a big hurricane flooded and washed away many roads. It was intense and lasted for at least three days. There was a very tall coconut tree in the front yard. The lightning struck it and it caught on fire. Despite all the rain, the fire kept burning but did not consume the tree. After the hurricane, a lot of people had to climb onto their housetops because of the flooding.

I am not sure why, but I had to go into town with my uncle's wife. Some parts of the road were submerged, and it was challenging for the big trucks that were transporting so many people and food. I remember we all had to go to one side of the truck so all our weight could hold the truck wheel down as the road had been partially washed away during the hurricane.

My stay with my uncle did not last long. Soon I was

back in hospital. But I never saw Antony again. I can only think he didn't make it. Rosie and Gilda were with me, but Rosie was getting weaker. Another girl from my community joined the group. She was not as sick and not as bedridden. Early in the mornings we would get a wheelchair, go outside, and pick up any mangoes that had fallen off the mango tree.

When I left hospital this time, I did not go back to my uncle. I was sent to a rich, white West Indian family, along with my mother's younger sister. They were quite a big family, originally from the Grand Cayman Islands. The husband was the head pastor of our community church and all the other branches of the church. This was the best home I stayed in. It was safe and had the best of everything. I shared a beautiful room with my aunt, who looked after me but also worked for the family. I went to school every day as they ran their own school and church, all of it on the same property as their house. Although it was not close to the hospital, it was lush, green flatland, not in the hottest part of Jamaica. I was happy there but did not see my mother. And it was too far for my sister to visit.

This happy experience came to an end when I went back into hospital. My heart had deteriorated badly. It was now a matter of when I would die. Neither Rosie nor Gilda was there on this stay, so it looked as if my three best friends had not made it. I asked the nurses, and they said my friends wouldn't be coming back to hospital again. In my heart, I knew what that meant. The other girl from my community was there with me for a short time, but then she went home, leaving me on the ward with just young babies.

As I got much sicker, Dr Angus spoke to my mother

about taking me to the United States as people there were preparing pioneering open-heart valve replacement operations. The doctor thought I would be a good candidate. She told my mother that I was going to die whether they tried to do something or not. This was a big decision for my mother to make, so she wrote to my dad. He had no problem in trying something, but he was not happy for me to go to the United States on my own as I would not have anyone there to keep an eye on me. My big brother had left the United States and was with my dad and my second-eldest brother in England. My dad made some enquiries and found out that they were looking for children who needed heart valve replacements in England, so he decided to get me over to England and into hospital there.

The hospital that was looking for children with my condition was not in the city where my dad and brothers lived. But the Justice of the Peace from our community had a niece who lived in England with her husband. They were visiting at the time, so my mother asked the niece if she would receive me in England and register me with her general practitioner so that I could get admitted into hospital. She agreed, so my mother started to make arrangements. I was removed from hospital for a day to have my passport picture taken and to go to the passport office. Then I returned to hospital to wait.

Chapter 3

The Journey to England

My mother did not tell me the whole plan. She just said that I was going to England to be with my father. That was not really so. One afternoon she turned up and took me to some house where there were lots of activities going on. By evening there was loud music and lots of people drinking, dancing, and talking. The lady in the house we were in was packing big suitcases; my mother had already packed a suitcase for me.

I did not get much sleep that night. In the morning, my mother, the lady, and I left the house. When we got to the airport, I remembered it was where I last had seen my father. A very tall gentleman came with a wheelchair for me. It was becoming clear to me that the lady whose house we stayed at would be travelling with me to England to be with my father. I was carried up the stairs and into the big bird by the tall man. There were so many people inside the big bird.

They settled me into a strange seat and fastened a belt around me. The lady who had accompanied me sat next to me. When the big bird took off, I had a strange feeling as we climbed high into the sky. I did not know what was at the other end waiting for me, but I was sure my father would be there.

I slept through the flight and when I awoke, they

announced that we would land in England soon. As the big bird prepared to come down out of the sky, I managed to look out of the window. All I could see were white clouds. Then the big bird started rocking from side to side, and many people looked frightened. But I was excited because I was close to seeing my father.

When the big bird finally came out of the sky and touched down on the ground, I looked out of the window. There were white clouds on the ground, and it felt cold. The big bird moved along the ground before finally coming to a stop. After a while, passengers were allowed to get up, gather their things, and leave. The lady and I were asked to wait. Then a white man came and put me in a wheelchair. I had seen white people before, but never so many, and I had never felt cold like that before.

We went through different processes before we got out to a place where crowds of people were standing and waiting. I looked and looked to see if I could see my father as this was where he would be waiting for me. But I was soon disappointed as a lady I had never seen before came to collect me. We got into the car she had waiting.

We were both quiet during our journey. I can't remember if she told me her name. I was numb. I could not even cry. I did not even take notice of the surroundings we were driving through. When we got to our destination and got out of the car, I had never seen houses like the ones the car stopped in front of. They were not made like the houses in Jamaica.

It was cold, there was no sun, and nothing looked like or reminded me of Jamaica. There were stairs inside the house. A lady came to say hello, but I did not say much in reply. As the day came to an end, her husband came home. At bedtime, for the whole time I spent there, I had to share a bed with them. But I never heard them having sex.

The first morning waking up in this new land was so cold. My father still hadn't shown up, so I did what I did best—I shut down my thinking and just observed.

The lady's husband left early to go to work and I realised there were more people using the other rooms upstairs. There was a toilet in the house, along with a bath. There was a black lady with a white husband and their black daughter, Paula, who was about one year older than me. Paula had her own room. She and I got on straightaway. She had to go to school but said that we could play as soon as she came home.

The lady I was staying with took me downstairs to stay with the lady I had met when I first arrived. She was a childminder and I would help her with the children, then when my new friend Paula came home, we would play. The family had this box called a television that showed real people. I enjoyed watching the television. It was a bit like the radio that I was used to, but with pictures.

Paula's dad was not her real father but her stepdad. I did not ask her any questions about her real dad as her stepdad was so loving. He drove a car, and they did things as a family. They allowed me to go along with them to the zoo park and sometimes to the market. My walking was stronger, and I really forgot about my sickness.

One evening when the lady I was staying with came home, she took me to the doctor's office, which was the house next door to where we were living. I saw a nurse and was registered with the doctor so I could get to the hospital.

It all seemed like a long time since I had arrived from Jamaica to this dark and gloomy country. I had expected my father to be waiting for me. One day I was doing my daily routine and helping the childminder with the children, when the doorbell rang. As the lady was feeding a small baby, she asked me to answer the door. She could see me from where she was sitting.

When I opened the door, there standing before me was my father. We looked at each other and my heart stopped beating. He took his hat off and said, "I am your father." Once my feet unfroze, I turned around, ran upstairs to the room I shared, and hid behind the bedhead. I could hear my heart beating loudly and fast.

I don't know how long I was behind the bed, but I do know that time seemed to stand still. At one point I heard footsteps coming up the stairs and a knock on the door. My father's voice called to me, "Norma, it's your father." I thought, *Yes, I know who you are. Why don't you just go away?*

But he didn't. He pushed the door open just as I was peeping from around the bedhead. He saw where I was hiding and tried to encourage me to come to him, but I would not leave my hiding place. He said I should tell the lady I was staying with that he had come to visit and would write to her. He waited for a few moments and then went back downstairs.

I heard him talking to the childminder as I peeped around the door. I saw her with him at the front door, and then he left. My heart fell, and the tears came. I stayed in the room for the rest of the day, until Paula came home from school.

Then one morning the lady asked me to get dressed for going out. I saw her packing a bag with some of my things. She was just as bad as my parents, never telling me what we were doing or where we were going.

That morning we got on a bus. At the end of the journey, we walked into a children's hospital, where they checked me in. I was back in a wheelchair and was taken to a small side ward with no one my age, just small children. And so the journey of the hospital began again.

The next morning, I saw the lady I was staying with. She was cleaning the hospital ward, but she never spoke to me, just looked at me. She did this every day except on her day off.

They started doing all kinds of tests on me. I was back on some injections that I had taken before in Jamaica. There was no one to talk to apart from the nurses when they came to feed the babies. They would come in to give me a bed bath, a bedpan, my injections, food, or to take blood. I also got to exchange a few words when the doctors came to do their rounds. Going for the tests was welcome as it would get me away from the ward.

One Sunday, I had a visit from my father, my eldest brother, my second-eldest brother, and my uncle. I did not look at my father and we could not find much to talk about. My eldest brother and I had nothing to say to each other either. But I talked to my second-eldest brother as we had always been close. They had brought me a doll and a colouring book. My uncle was not a talkative man; he just looked at me as if I were some pet in a cage.

But it was very good to see my second-eldest brother. I had so many questions for him. I had completely closed my heart to my father. He found it very difficult to reach out and hug me, when that's all I wanted from him. All my feelings were locked away so tightly, and I did not have anyone to talk to; no one had ever asked, and I never knew how to say what I felt. I just learned to survive, take care of myself, and deal with my pain and discomfort. I never complained or cried. I learned not to get attached to anyone as I was always on the move. People came and went. I never had friends for long periods and had to quickly adjust to my situations as they changed. When it was time for my family to leave, I was sad to see them go, but mostly I would miss my second-eldest brother.

I stayed in hospital for some months. Then one morning, they packed my belongings, and I was put in an ambulance. I was driven to a convalescent home in Surrey. The home was on a large section of farmland. There were horses and fields with trees and walking tracks. The other children and I were about the same age. We had bikes to ride, and they also allowed us to ride the horses.

My stay there was the best. The place had a schoolroom, and if you were not feeling well, a teacher would come to your bed. This was the most schooling I had ever had. We only had school in the morning. After lunch we all had to sleep until afternoon tea, and then we would play until supper time. I had good days and bad days, but the fresh air, perfect environment, and happy days helped me to get stronger.

One evening I was taken to the office and given the phone. On the other end of the phone was my mother. She was in England with my eldest sister. It felt good to hear my mother's voice, though as usual, she did not tell me anything. I had gotten very used to living life without my family. I did not build up my hopes for anything and had no emotions when hearing from my mother. I did not ask her any questions about me going home. My family had all become strangers to me. I never had another phone call from my mother while I was at the convalescent home.

Chapter 4

The Day I Changed the World

One day the convalescent home packed up my things and I saw that an ambulance was waiting for me. I didn't know where I was going, but I got in. At the end of the journey, we stopped outside a house and my father came out to meet the ambulance. I discovered that this was where my mother, father, and sister lived.

Later that evening, I found out that my eldest brother and second-eldest brother lived two doors away. My dad worked nights and my mother worked days, and my eldest sister was already going to senior school. Our living conditions were far from what we had in Jamaica. Even though this house was bigger than our house in Jamaica, all we had to live in was one room in the house, which was shared. In the room was a double bed, a sofa bed, and a tall kitchen cabinet. My sister and I slept on the sofa bed. All our possessions were in this one room. My brothers came to join us for breakfast and dinner.

The toilet was outside. We kept a pail under the bed to urinate or poo in if we had to at night. Then in the morning, we emptied it out in the toilet. We also had a big washbasin. On Saturdays my mother heated water and filled the basin for the three of us to take baths in the same water. I would get the first bath as I was the youngest and my body was not so dirty. Then it was my sister's turn, and then my mother's. My father and brothers went to the local swimming bath to have a shower. All the men in the community did that on Saturdays. The swimming bath was just at the top of the road we lived on.

There was only one stove in the kitchen, and everyone who lived in the house could only use one burner at a time on the stove as everyone was usually cooking at the same time. The food was taken to the bedrooms and kept in the kitchen cabinet.

Some evenings my parents had prayer meetings in our room with some friends they had made.

The house we lived in was owned by an Indian man. He had the big living room opposite the kitchen and next to the door that led outside to the yard and toilet. He lived in the room with his wife, son, brother, and nephew. There was another big room downstairs where a black family lived, a husband, wife, and young daughter. Our room was upstairs. Across the landing from our room was another black couple's room; they had no kids.

I had to stay with my father during the day, but he slept most of the day, so I had to be quiet. There was nothing for me to do. When he woke up, he would make me something to eat. Then he would cook dinner. The kitchen was not busy during the day, so dinner would be ready for the rest of the family when they got home. There was a little black-and-white television in our room, but my father only switched it on to watch the news and then would switch it off. We never had a radio, so there was not much to do. My sister was lucky because she had her homework to do. But on Saturdays, she had to go with my mother to the launderette to wash everyone's clothes and to the grocery to do the weekly shopping.

I thought I was home for good, but I spent only two weeks with my family before my parents packed my bag and we went on a long coach journey. They did not tell me where we were going, but I guessed it was some hospital as my parents had their friends praying for me one night.

We arrived at a hospital in Leeds. It was a bright, beautiful city. There were plenty of daffodils all over the city. My parents checked me into the hospital and this time, my mother did not hide and run away. When I was settled, they said goodbye and left. I was on a long ward. Four boys around my age were already on the ward, along with some young babies.

One of the boys was so ill that it was difficult for us to get to know him properly as his parents spent a lot of time with him. Eventually, his parents decided to take him to the United States, where they were already carrying out experiments on the heart valve. I never knew the outcome of this boy's life.

The other boys and I became good friends. They shared information with me, so I was beginning to understand more about this stay in hospital.

Because I was mobile, I would go to the adult ward. At that time, the wards were mixed, men on one side and women on the other side. I spent most of the day helping out on the adult ward, fetching books and magazines and running any other little errands l could for the patients.

The adults on the ward had plenty of information on me and the boys waiting for our operations. They knew it was an experimental operation. I would hear them talking. They would say, "Poor loves." Over the years, I had mastered the art of not thinking, and that's what I did. If it was happening, it was not happening to me.

The first experimental operation was done on one of the boys. We watched as he was taken to the theatre on the morning of his operation. His parents were with him too.

After some days, or maybe weeks—it seemed to be a long time—they brought him back to the ward. He seemed to be doing well, but one night he started to feel really unwell. One thing I had learned from my stays in hospital was not to sleep deeply at night as it always seemed to be in the night when sick people became acutely unwell. So I heard him struggling and called for the nurse. When the nurses arrived, they called for the emergency team with machines. The doctor pulled the screen around the boy's bed. It seemed like they worked on him for hours. Then they took the machines away but left the screen around his bed. They told me they had given him something so he could sleep. I fell back to sleep, but I heard the nurses come back and give him a wash, so I thought he must be doing OK. I took my mind off him and slept. By the time I woke up in the morning, he was gone and his bed was neatly made. When the nurse came, I asked her where he was. She said that because he was not well, they had to take him back to the ward where he could receive the special care he needed. I never believed that story as I knew about death, and that boy never came back to the ward. The adults were very cagey but the news had spread that the operation was not successful.

After some time, the other two boys went for their operations. They never came back to the ward, so I had no idea how long they lived after their operations. We were all very sick and would have died with or without the operation. I just never thought about it as I never knew what was behind dying. I did not know where people really went when they died, except for what I had seen my relatives doing to my two grandmothers' bodies, putting them each in a box and putting the boxes in the ground.

I did not allow any fear or feelings to come into my head. I just enjoyed every day, doing little things for the adult patients who appreciated my help. Their visitors would bring me sweets and colouring books.

I knew my turn for surgery was near as the whispering on the adult ward started again. "Poor love, it's her turn soon." Then one Saturday, I had a visit from my parents and they spoke to the doctors. I had no idea what the conversation was about, but I now know it was to sign the consent forms for me to have the operation and to choose the type of valve they wished the doctors to use for my replacement. It was something that my older brothers and sister would talk about over the years. My parents had a choice of a pig heart valve or a plastic heart valve, and as my parents did not eat pig because of their religious beliefs, they chose the plastic heart valve. They did not visit with me for long, but that was not unusual.

By Sunday, there was no hiding the moods of the patients on the adult ward, so I decided to ask my favourite nurse what was happening. She told me that on Monday morning, I would be going to have my operation. She said I could have anything I wanted for my Sunday dinner. Everyone seemed to be in a more fearful mood than I. All I was thinking was, *there is no way I am going to die like the others did. I did not come from Jamaica just to die here.*

I remained with a stillness within myself and ate all the ice cream I could manage on that Sunday.

I slept well that Sunday night knowing that in the morning, I would be experiencing the same operation as the boys on my ward. I had no idea that I would be put to sleep. I had no expectations of the procedure and no knowledge that they were going to cut me open.

I woke up to a beautiful Monday morning. By this time, it was only the small babies on the ward with me. My favourite nurse was feeding a baby, and I asked her if she would accompany me to the theatre. She said yes. I was given a shower and was not allowed anything to eat or drink. They gave me an injection that made me feel sleepy by the time the porter came for me and by the time we got to the lifts, I was asleep.

The next time I woke up I was on a dimly lit ward with all kinds of tubes coming from me and a nurse calling my name, telling me to wake up. I awoke, but all I wanted to do was sleep, so she let me. I don't know how long I slept, but the next time I awoke, I was more conscious that I was alive and had had the operation. I was not in any pain or feeling any discomfort. My breathing was easy, and my heart was not beating loudly in my ear. A nurse was by my bed. She gave me some water to drink and said that my parents had called and sent their love. There were two get-well cards on the locker by my bed. I remember one was from my dad, and the other was from the patients on the adult ward where I spent most of my days. The nurses read them both to me.

I don't know how long I spent on the special ward,

but I got stronger every day. One day they allowed me back on the original ward. It felt good to see my special nurse. I was not allowed out of bed, but I was in good spirits. My parents never came to see me, but I am sure they would have called to check on my progress. I slept a lot, and as I had no one to talk to, my healing time was spent observing myself and talking to myself, knowing that my life had changed. I was going to live a normal life and be able to do normal things.

I was conscious of what had happened to the other boy when he came back to the ward. I am not sure how many days after I returned to the ward that I had the same experience he had, but I do know that my experience started off much different from his.

I awoke to the most beautiful sunny morning. The night nurses had gone, and my favourite nurse was to my right, feeding the same baby she had fed the morning I had surgery. The morning was still as I looked out the window. The sky was a perfect blue, with fluffy white clouds passing by slowly and gently. My body felt light and healthy, as if I was a newborn who had never been ill. I could hear all the sounds around me. Though there were no birds at the window, I could still hear them harmonising loudly. I could hear the sounds of different harmonies in the spaces where it looked as if there was nothing, and when I looked at the sky, I could even hear the harmony coming from the sky. Everything around me had a harmony; there was even harmony from my bed sheets. I turned to my favourite nurse and asked her if she could hear music. She said no. I told her I was well, that there was nothing wrong with me anymore, and that I wanted to go home. She told me that when the doctor came to see me I was to tell him how well I was feeling.

A nurse came in to give me my tablets and an injection. I told her I did not want any more injections as I was not sick anymore. She told me, "Let's do this one, and you can tell the doctor you don't want injections anymore." She gave me the injection, and for the first time since my illness, I did not feel it. After giving me the injection, the nurse picked up my chart at the end of my bed. As she turned the pages of the chart, it played a harmony that sounded like a violin. I asked her if she could hear the music that the chart was playing.

When she left, I turned to my favourite nurse, who was still feeding the baby, and said, "I am well, and I am going home now." I threw the sheets off me, pulled myself up, and holding onto the bedrails, started to get out of my bed. I heard my favourite nurse shout, "No, Norma. Don't get out of bed."

But I found myself standing on the floor and holding onto the bed. My ankles started to buckle, and I collapsed. I felt myself totally separated from my body. I started floating above my body and heard the panic of my favourite nurse calling for help from the doctor and the crash team. I was given an oxygen mask, and the adrenaline injection. I tried to tell them I was not going to die, but they could not hear me. Then my harmony drifted back into my body, and I slowly woke up.

From that day, my progress just got better and better. I began needing fewer injections and fewer tablets. My stitches were removed, all sixty-seven of them. I had been stitched up with black thread. My scar went from the middle of my chest around my right breast and up and around to the middle of my back. I found out later that one of my ribs had also been removed. This style of surgery made my recovery quicker as there was no healing of the breastbone. But still, my parents did not come to see me.

This new me felt as if I had not been sick for the past few years. I was now confident, healthy, and walking strong. The patients on the adult ward were amazed. Everyone was delighted, and my doctors were over the moon. I was now well enough to leave the hospital and was sent to a beautiful convalescent home in Stratford-upon-Avon with lots of happy children. We played all day and walked through beautiful fields. But still my parents never came to visit me.

I was at the convalescent home for quite some time, being monitored and checked by my doctors, who came down from Leeds to see me. Then one day they said I could go home, but my parents never came to get me, so I was taken home in an ambulance.

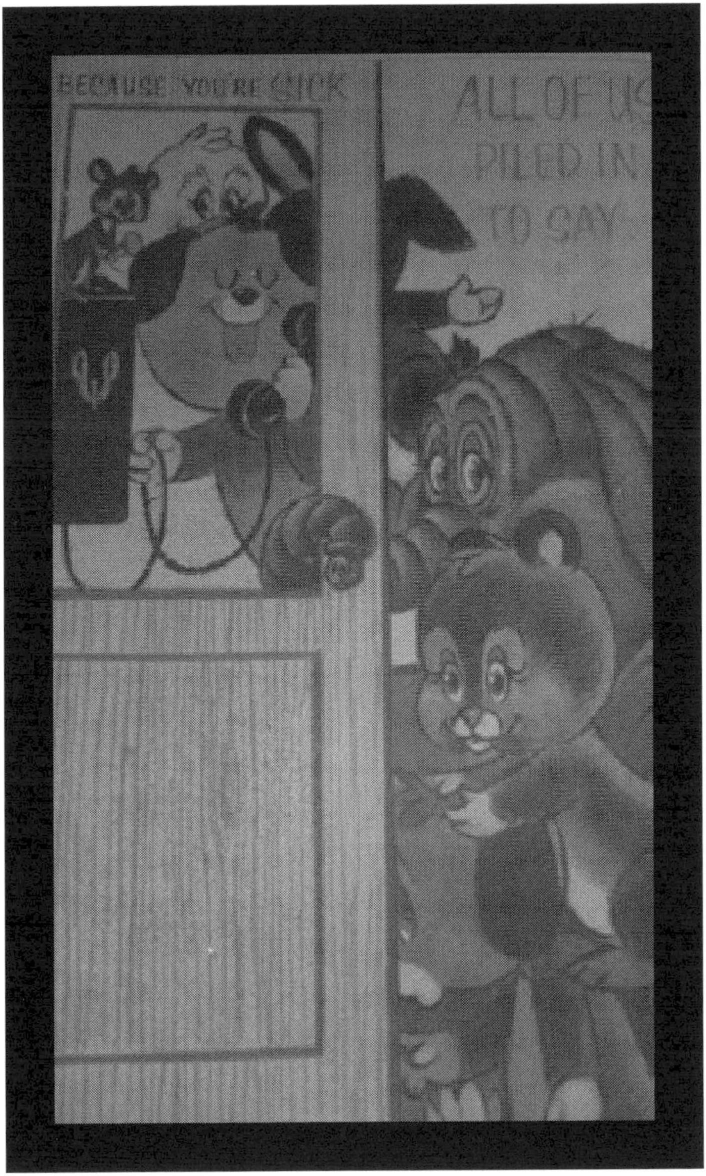
BECAUSE YOU'RE SICK
ALL OF
PILED IN
TO SAY

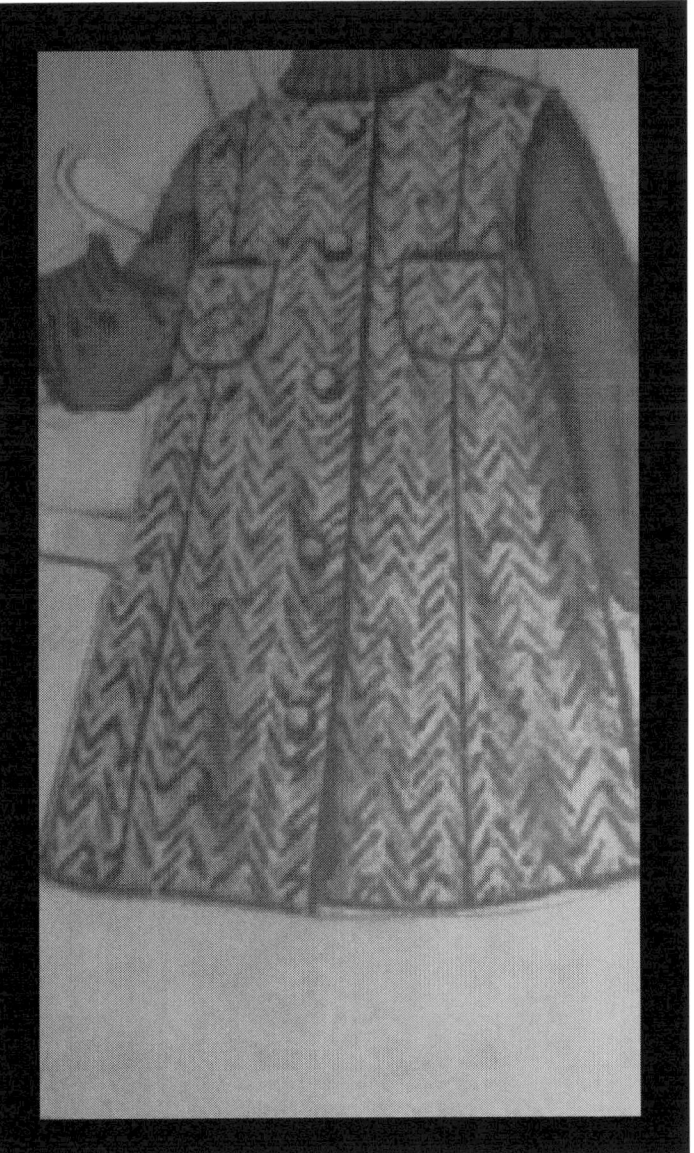

Chapter 5
Schooldays

After I was reunited with my family, I did not attend school for some time. During the day, as my father slept, I hung out with the little girl who lived downstairs with her family. One evening, I was playing with the little girl as she rode her tricycle in the passage and into the kitchen area. The room door of the Indian family's home was open, and there was the son, the brother, the brother's son, the husband, and the wife all watching television. The wife and husband were on the bed, lying under their duvet, and the husband was clearly having sex while drinking a can of beer and watching television, laughing. When the beer was finished, she got up to get him another beer. When she returned, she resumed her position. But the duvet slipped off and exposed them. The little girl saw all this and was curious, so she asked the son what his father was doing to his mother. He said, "My father sex my mother." Then he asked the little girl, "Your mommy and daddy don't sex?" The little girl rode off laughing.

I also made friends with a girl my age who lived across the road, next to the junior school she attended. She would come over after school and play with me till her mother came home from work. I found her amazing as she was able to do the splits and wrap her legs around her body. She was so flexible that she was able to get into all kinds of positions with her body.

Living in an Indian house was interesting, but it came with its challenges, especially living in one room with four people and doing everything in one space, especially with having two others for dinner.

Just before I started junior school, a couple, who were my parents' church friends, convinced them to let me come and stay with them. The lady had just had her baby, which would be company for me and her during the day. I thought it would be better than hanging around the house while my dad slept. I had to sleep with the couple at night and was put in the middle.

Finally, I was allowed to start junior school, but not at the school across the road from where we lived. That one was full, so I went to another junior school, about a fifteen-minute walk from home. There were not many black children at the school, but we all became friends, and some of the white girls played with me. I had no problems at junior school and spent happy days learning and playing. I went home for my lunch, and Dad prepared something for me to eat.

My days at junior school only lasted for a year. During that summer's holidays, my father bought a house just off the road we were living on. It was a big house with a large garden that led to an unused train line. There was a big cellar, two large storage rooms, and a toilet in a kind of conservatory, all leading from the kitchen. A dining room, large reception room, and front room were downstairs. Upstairs were two large bedrooms rooms, a medium-sized room, a box room, a toilet, and a bathroom. We had two tenant families: a wife and husband with no kids downstairs, and upstairs, a wife and husband with two small boys. My two brothers had the medium-sized room. My sister and I shared the box room, and my parents took the other big room.

The lady my parents had bought the house from was a teacher, and her husband had died in the house. My younger sister, my younger brother, and I always had the feeling that the husband's spirit was still in the house. I know I saw him on lots of occasions, but he never interfered with any of us. He just watched.

Among our neighbours were a white doctor and his wife. They had two sons, a car, and a beautiful dog. Another neighbour was a black family with one girl and two boys, and they kept a couple of bad dogs. There were quite a few other black families who lived on our street, and more came the longer we lived there. At the top of the street was a big house. We thought it was a school as many young boys and girls were taken there during the day, so we called it the "bad school for naughty children". Years later, I learned it was a psychiatric evaluation centre.

When I was growing up in England, the summer was guaranteed to be hot but winter was cold with snow almost knee-high and plenty of fog. To me, spring was the most special though.

It felt very good to live in our own house. Our garden was so big that my dad was able to grow many different vegetables. We had a greenhouse, a beautiful rose garden, and an immaculate lawn. My sister and I had chores to do that were mostly done on a Saturday. I had to sweep the stairs, mop the passage, and polish the floor tiles. My sister had to wash everyone's clothes. I had to help her as we didn't have a washing machine. We did get one eventually, but my mother always said it never washed her whites clean enough, so we still had to wash those by hand. I also had to do all the dusting in my parents' room, my brothers' room, and the front room. The front room was full of ornaments and lots of plastic flowers with elaborate crocheted place mats. We were cautioned not to break anything as if we were to do so, we would have to save up our pocket money and replace any items we had broken.

The family who lived upstairs always had some drama going on. The husband was good-looking and was always out. He also came home drunk sometimes. They fought, and the two boys would cry—one for Mommy, and one for Daddy—to stop fighting. Sometimes the wife took all her husband's best clothes and threw them out the window.

In September, I started secondary school. A uniform was a must, so my father bought it for me. The skirts were very long and the blazers so much bigger than me. My father said I would grow into them but I never did, so I had to roll the skirt up at the waist not to look odd.

The boys' secondary school was joined on to the girls' school. They divided the playground with rails. At break time, lunchtime, and when school was over, the boys were let out ten minutes before the girls.

There were only a handful of black girls and boys at secondary school. All the girls, black and white, who went to my junior school with me went to the same secondary school I attended. There were no black boys at junior school, but by the time we got to secondary school there were already some older black boys and some new ones in my year. My eldest sister was already going to the same secondary school with three other black girls in her year. They had only one year left before leaving school. As the years went by, more black boys, black girls, and Indian children made up the population of my secondary school.

There was a black girl I used to play with at junior school, but she was two years younger than me. When I got to secondary school, her older brother, who was two years older than me, went to the boys' school. Their house was on the street next to the school, and if I took the shortcut home, I would have to pass their house. And, boy, I fell in love with him.

Ryan was tall and handsome. He would never talk. He just looked. He had a brand-new bicycle that he looked magnificent on. Every night I dreamed of him, me, and our children—and we were very rich. When I saw him, my heart would stop beating. But he just ignored me and seemed to look straight through me. If I was on my way to school by myself and I saw him, he just slowly rode past me to wind me up.

All the boys at school and in my neighbourhood had the hots for me, but I was not interested in them. So one Valentine's Day, they played a trick on me. They gave me a Valentine card and said that Ryan had given it to them to give to me. They also gave him one that was supposed to be from me. It was so hurtful. I went to talk to Ryan, who was on his bike, and he tried to run me over.

All my black friends and I went home for lunch as we did not like the school food, but we stayed on Fridays, like we did at junior school, as it was fish and chips and apple pie or crumble with custard.

It was at secondary school that I experienced racism. Even my white friend I played with at junior school started acting racist. We started fighting in the playground one day in the winter. There was deep snow and we were throwing snowballs at each other. Something possessed her to add a stone to the snowball. It hit me very hard in my eyes. Luckily, it only made me see flashing lights and did not cause any permanent damage. Of course, it started an argument between us when the pain wore off. She called me a *black bastard*. But just as I was going to fight her, the bell rang, and she ran to class.

We sat beside each other in class, and I was not afraid of my teacher. In those days, we had to write with black fountain pens, and on each desk was a fountain pot that could be removed to fill up with ink. The inkpot was full that day, so when we settled down, I took it out and threw the black ink in my friend's face. Her face went black, and the ink dripped down her white blouse. I asked her, "Who is a black bastard now?" Of course, I was sent to the headmistress' office, lost three points for my house team, and got double detention. Did I care that she had hurt me physically? To me, that was more painful than being called a black bastard, and all the punishment was worth it to set a precedent that I would not be bullied, not even by a friend. She and I stopped being friends, and I no longer sat with her in class.

We black girls were always challenged in the playground as the white girl bullies wanted to show us as what they called "the cock of the school". We stuck together as black girls; you could say it was our gang. We were challenged to fight every day in the playground. We always travelled to and from school together, even at break times. If one of us stayed at school for lunch on a Friday, we all stayed.

Sometimes we took the bus home But other times we walked the normal way home or took shortcuts. On our way home from school one evening we took one of the shortcuts and this lone white boy rode up to us and spewed chewed-up peanuts all over us. It went in our faces, over our anoraks, and in our hair. And it stank.

We observed his movements and knew that he rode one of the shortcut routes to his house for lunch, so we planned an ambush for a lunchtime. We all gathered small stones, and each of us hid in a front garden, behind the wall of a house on the street. As the boy got to the middle of the ambush, we stoned him. He fell off his bike, and we all punched him. He made sure not to cross us again.

One of our biggest fights was in the back playground. It was started by the white girls who were the school bullies. One was tall and we had a tall black girl in our group, so the two of them were matched to fight. But during the lunchtime fight, the white girl's boyfriend turned up and started fighting our friend. He pulled a knife, and we all jumped on him. We held onto his leg and grabbed his cock, squeezing it until he backed down. Lucky for us, a male teacher, seeing the fight from his classroom, came out and broke it up. He reported the white girl and her boyfriend, and they were both expelled from school. This made our lives much easier as the other white girls now knew who the real cocks of the school were. We settled down in school and were comfortable playing boyfriend and girlfriend with our black boys.

The gang culture was still in motion outside the school and in our communities. There were white gangs known as skinheads and Teddy Boys who attacked young black and Indian men. They would burn down the Indian men's shops. This movement created the black gang culture as it was the only way for black men to survive. The skinheads and the Teddy boys were rival gangs, and they also had gang fights with each other.

I still got into trouble at school. As West Indian families, we never cooked the foods white British people cooked, so we never had the same ingredients in our parents' cupboards. My problem was with cookery class. My mother would never buy the ingredients I asked her to buy for my cookery class as the family food budget would not stretch, and I did not want to take my pocket money to buy them. When I did manage to get the ingredients for the cookery class, I took the finished product home and no one would eat it, so I would have to throw it away. My second-eldest brother would tell me not to bring that mess home, so if I cooked at class, I had to throw the food away before I got home. If it was biscuits or small cakes, I would share them with the black boys on our way home from school.

On the days when I could not bring ingredients for cookery class, I had to do maths outside the headmistress' office, and the corridor was very cold in the winter. When I started to resist, they would say I had to scrub the school corridor floor and would give me a bucket and scrubbing brush. This meant I would have to get down on my knees to scrub, and I was not going to start that rubbish. So I filled the bucket with water and poured it from the top of the corridor until it was flooded. This was what all the students had to face after class.

Before I got to secondary school, my dream was to become a doctor as I had spent so much time in hospital. But that dream was soon forgotten as there were so many distractions at school, and teachers were not interested in teaching black children, whether we did well or not. And our parents left it up to the school, so we were never encouraged at home or in school. And I was busy trying to break all the rules as I had never had to deal with so many rules and so much discipline.

After Ryan left school, I enjoyed the attention of other boys. I never allowed any of them to kiss me and never did anything inappropriate with any of them, apart from being flirtatious. Years later I saw Ryan, and I was glad he never liked me. He matured into an ugly man, not my type.

The strangest thing happened in my third year. The boys' and girls' school combined. One day a new boy joined the class. To my surprise, it was Campbell, whom I had gone to school with in Jamaica. The other children used to tease me on the way home from school, saying I was going home to cook my husband dinner, as he had taken a shine to me. Not only was he in my class, but also his big sister, Pam, was my best friend—and his stepfather was my father's distant cousin, so he was allowed to come to our house.

One of the things that my mother never allowed us to do was to talk to boys or have them as friends. On Saturday afternoons, when my mother came home from work, I would have to go shopping with her and pull the shopping trolley. I always saw boys from school with their moms, pulling shopping trolleys. I could never say hello to them, even if our mothers knew each other and stopped for a chat. Sometimes they would catch me being slapped in my mouth by the back of my mother's hand if I asked her to buy me something. If she said no and I sulked, I would get her backhand. By the time I got to school on Monday morning, the news would be all over the school. We never had mobile phones at that time, but it seemed as if nothing was missed.

My parents were still involved with the same people who had come to the house to pray and have church, but now they had another place to hold their church services, so they weren't using our house. Every Sunday we would make the long journey by bus to church. At first the pastor who had a car picked us up, but that stopped as the bus had a route close to our house that stopped within walking distance to the church. Sometimes at night, if we missed the last bus because church went on late, the pastor would give us a lift home. The church had a van that transported church members and Sunday school children who lived more locally.

My best friend at church was Wendy. She had two older sisters and a younger brother. I would ask my mother to let me have Sunday dinner at her house. My parents had their own friends whose house we went to for Sunday dinner, but it was boring for me as they didn't have any children at that time. My older sister was best friends with one of Wendy's sisters, and as we only saw each other on Sundays, we had lots to catch up on. There were plenty of other girls and boys our age at church, and we were watched by the pastor's wife, to whom they gave the title "mother of the church", along with some other mothers if their husbands were deacons. My father was a deacon, so my mother also had the mother title, along with Wendy's mother. Wendy's parents were really cool and not strong disciplinarians like my mother was. They had a selection of board games that I loved to play. Their father was very interested in their education, and they all turned out to be high achievers. Years later, the younger brother became my son's godfather.

Wendy and I loved to sing, so we decided that we would form a group. We asked two sisters to join us. They agreed. We became the *Gospel Singers*. As the church service was held in a school hall, we would practise in the toilets for the evening service. The church would give us a spot to sing. As more people joined the church with their children, if the children were girls and we became friends with them, we asked them to join our group. We sang for big programmes, such as when the church had its annual convention, when we would get together with other branches of the church.

This was an exciting time for us as we were stars. The older boys who backed us playing the guitars, drum, and piano were older and sexy—I had my favourite—and it was exciting to watch them onstage. The pastor's wife formed a youth choir that I was also part of, so I got to sing twice at conventions or at our church.

There was a boy from one of the bigger churches who liked me. He was not what I wanted, but I enjoyed flirting with him and knowing how much he liked me. Wendy and I wrote letters to each other during the week, and once my mother opened one of them. We were just talking about the boys at the convention. And what did my mother do? She took the letter and showed it to the pastor's wife. They made a big thing about it. Wendy's mother was cool and did not make a fuss like my mother and the pastor's wife.

My dislike for the pastor's wife started to grow, she manipulated a lot of the girls who were not very strong. Sometimes on a Sunday she would get us all to have dinner at her house and teach us how to be Christian young ladies. She got the girls she could manipulate to tell her what we were talking about and then would use it against us.

I loved singing and wanted to do some song writing. My eldest brother taught piano lessons in the evenings, and I was one of his students.

I sang lead in the school choir, and the husband of a lady at church played guitar in a well-known band. He started to attend the church and play in the church band. Then one day he brought the most handsome young man I had seen since I'd fallen out of love with Ryan. His name was Earl. He was about nineteen or twenty and very experienced with things of the world. He also played in the band. I fell in love with him instantly, And I knew he liked me. I started to practise with Earl and the lady's husband on Wednesday nights before the church service. It was a different kind of music and included songs I wrote. Earl and I started showing up much earlier for practice so we could be alone. Then the pastor's wife saw how much I was into him and embarrassed me on a few occasions. Knowing this, I got Earl to hug me one night on the church altar so that when they were having service, I would think of being hugged on their precious altar and feel powerful.

We had a phone at home, but I was not allowed

to make calls. And if a friend was going to call, we would have to arrange a time so I could run to answer the phone. My parents could never know it was a boy who called me. Earl called me in the evenings. I was very much in love with him. He convinced me to go out on a date with him one evening. So on an evening when I was supposed to be at night school learning shorthand and typing, I did not go. Instead, I went to meet Earl.

When I got to the meeting place, he was driving a big white van and had a friend with him. I got into the van, and he drove to some backstreet. With his friend staying in the front, Earl and I got out. He took me to the back of the van, which was clearly the transport the band used for their equipment. Earl tried to have sex with me but I was not having it as before he had told me I was too young for him and decided he could not see me anymore. But now he said we should have sex to remember each other. I loved sex, but I was not stupid. I got out of the van and ran crying all the way to the bus stop. Luckily, the bus came quickly, and I cried all the way home.

I never saw or heard from Earl again. I was sick for weeks. I wanted to die as I was really growing up and experiencing emotions.

My eldest sister left school and went into nursing. She went far away, so she had to live in the nurses' home. By now my younger sister and brother had come from Jamaica, and both were going to the junior school. My eldest brother got married and left home. My second-eldest brother also left home and was living with his girlfriend, so my younger brother had the box room that my eldest sister and I used to share. My younger sister and I shared the room my older brothers used to have. The upstairs and downstairs tenants left, and after some time, my second-eldest brother moved back home. He had the room downstairs with his own television, which we still weren't allowed to watch. But we listened to the radio that was kept in our parents' room when they weren't about.

My mother's only brother and the mother of his children decided to marry. I was one of their bridesmaids. It was a big affair. Lots of my friends from school attended as it was more of a community affair. A very distant family member of my father's, who lived in a big city, was at the wedding. It was the first time I had met him. He was married with two older sons and asked my parents if I could come to stay with them during the long summer holiday. I convinced my parents to let me go. They did not know I was a very promiscuous girl, and l knew exactly what I was going for as l had already flirted with this man. My parents said yes.

I was around thirteen by then and had the experience of my life in the city. The wife was a pretty woman. She worked days, and the husband worked nights. Their two sons worked during the day. They were very handsome, tall boys. One slept downstairs and the other upstairs. Their parents' bedroom was upstairs, along with a small spare room where I stayed.

I spent two weeks with them, and boy, what an eventful two weeks they were. As soon as the wife left for work, her husband was in my bed, and he and I had sex several times before we got out of bed. Then he would take me to do some sightseeing around the city. Then during the night, the son who slept downstairs would climb up through my bedroom window, and he and I would have sex. And when he left, his brother came in, and I had more sex; I think they planned it. I hardly slept at night. Then in the morning, it was more sex with their father. This went on every night during my stay. I was sad to go home, but I went home on a high.

My second-eldest brother left home again and my eldest brother moved back in with his wife. Not long after, they had their first child. As I had to help with the baby, I got a chance to watch TV in their room.

I was still going to night school for shorthand and typing. A nightclub opened just two streets from where we lived and the opening time was eight in the evening. Night school started at seven and finished at nine, so I was expected home by ten. I could push it to ten-thirty by saying the bus was late or that it did not go all the way and we had to get off and walk. So what my cousin Pam and I did was to go to night school, sign in, and stay for half an hour. Our excuse was that the bus was getting us home too late, and our parents were not happy with us coming home so late. We would then get to the nightclub by eight-thirty. By that time, it was almost full as people went out early as entertainment places closed during the week at twelve. I would change into my dancing costume and was on the platform doing my go-go dancing. I was fourteen then. Lucky for us, in those days they did not check IDs. There was a local policeman there whom I regularly had sex with in alleyways. In the winter, it was dark and foggy when Pam and I came from night school. When I parted company with her—her street was after mine—I would hang around the street and offer sex to white men. I did so with this policeman, and he never said no.

Someone saw Pam and me either going in or coming out of the nightclub and told my father. One night as we came out of the nightclub, Pam said to me, "Don't look, but your father is across the street." In those days, girls always walked with their best friends, their arms tucked in each other's arms to show they were close. And that's how my cousin and I walked up the street, watching my dad walking quickly ahead of us. When we got to my street, she said, "You have to run away tonight. Come and stay at my house. You can hide there."

But I knew I had to face the music at some point, so I figured I might as well get it over and be done with it. By the time I got home, my father was in his room. He never said anything about seeing me coming out of the nightclub. He'd just wanted to see for himself.

I could not wait to leave school. Our school had joined with another school, and this did not encourage me to stay on at school to complete any qualifications. The leaving age was fifteen. I just wanted to grow up, make my own money, and leave home. I felt that my parents—especially my mother and her strict discipline—were getting in my way. And most of all, what right did she have, seeing as I had taken care of myself when I needed her the most? And now she wanted to get in my way of doing what I wanted to do. I could not wait to leave school. On the last day of school, I ran out of those school gates and never looked back.

Chapter 6
Falling in Love and
the Teenage Years

I finally left school at fifteen with no qualifications, but I managed to get a job in an office as a junior clerk with two days' release to go to college. I was the first black person whom the company had hired to work in its office. It was a manufacturing company that made oil seals. The factory workers were mostly Indians, with some West Indians and a few whites. The office staff that I was part of was quite small and the office manager was not much different from my school headmistress. I had to learn everyone's roles in the office and make tea and coffee.

Up front they all treated me nicely, but they acted different behind my back, so I had to be very careful and learn to play the game. I became good friends with Mary, the head typist. She was married but was up for having an affair if the right man were to come along. She invited me to her house a few times for dinner with her and her husband, and she went out many times with me and my cousin Pam to nightclubs.

My wages were three pounds twenty-five pence a week. I was allowed to open my wage packet, count the money to make sure it was right, close it up, and take it home to my mother. This was the English way. She would give me back twenty-five pence for my weekly expenses, such as any clothes and shoes I needed to buy, along with whatever else I might need.

By law I was not an adult until I was twenty-one, so I still had to find ways to do the adult things I wanted to do. I wanted to be a singer. There was a talent show on television called *Opportunity Knocks*, and they were holding auditions in a city not far from where l lived. I applied and was invited to the audition. Lucky for me, it was on one of the days I had college. That made it easy for me to take the day off to attend the audition. The song that I practised to sing was "I Don't Know How to Love Him" from the musical *Jesus Christ Superstar.*

The auditions started at nine in the morning, but I did not get a chance to sing till around eight in the evening. I was almost the last to audition. I was tired, hungry, and not at my best. The presenter of the show was Hughie Green, a lovely man. Even I knew my performance was not the best. I was not chosen for the show.

I did not dwell on being a singer for long. My mother was not happy about me being a singer as she said it was not to the glory of God.

One of my teachers at college was a handsome man. I had made friends with a Brazilian girl, and neither of us was doing well in his class. He approached us on our way home, and we took turns getting in his car to perform sexual favours for a passing mark in his class. I also asked him for gifts. He gave me a beautiful sapphire ring.

I also got busy with a young married draftsman, James, who worked at the office. I started making out with him in the stockroom. I knew Mary liked him, and they went out once for a drink, but as they both were married, it did not work out. I started to see

James outside of work, and he asked me if he could bring his best friend, Joe, so both of them could have sex with me. I was up for it, and we would all meet at least once a week. Joe was into making blue movies, and he shot one of me and James. Joe and I started hanging out without James, as it was difficult for James as a married man. Joe made a few blue movies of me and him. I never knew what he did with those movies.

I was constantly looking for excitement and decided that maybe I could make it as a Page 3 girl in *The Sun* newspaper. So I found a little old man who was a photographer and got him to do some topless and glam shots of me, but I did not take it any further.

By the time I was sixteen, I went to the Brook Clinic and got the pill. I was making all kinds of excuses not to go to church and finally, I refused to go altogether. On a Sunday, everyone, including my brother and his wife, went to church all day and stayed with friends for Sunday dinner, so I had the house to myself. I would go to this working man's club and strip for these dirty old white men who wanted to grope me. I also walked around the shopping centre on Sunday evenings to pick up men for sex.

I met Harry at the shopping centre on one of those Sunday evenings, and we started dating. He was older than me. One Sunday evening I took him back to the house and had sex with him on my parents' bed. I did it because I was having so many problems with my mother. She was constantly on my case. She even called the police on me to give me a warning. I wanted to have more freedom. I stopped going to night school, and my parents locked the front doors by ten at night. It did not give me enough time to stay out, so I had to find ways to get into the house at nights by getting my younger sister to sneak downstairs when my parents were asleep and unbolt the door.

Harry was a party guy. One night he took me to a pot and orgy party. I was the only black person there. They were smoking things I had no idea about, getting high, and having sex. The sex was more my kind of thing. I had so much sex that night.

Harry and I drifted apart and I started going to a nightclub outside my town where I met a guy who had a car, so I could get a ride home. And, of course, we had sex in his car. I could hardly call it sex as his penis was not even as big as my little finger.

I soon met another handsome white boy at this nightclub. Steve was divorced and from a wealthy background. He also had a small boat. We had fun. He asked me if I would have sex with three of his friends; they wanted to know what it was like to have sex with a black woman. I agreed, and Steve arranged for this to happen at his house. I had sex first with Steve, and then two of his friends did it with me. The third friend was not keen to do it with me, but the others talked him into it. Three days later, my vagina was on fire, itching and burning when I peed. I mentioned it to Pam, who was doing her nursing, and she told me I had to go to a special clinic at the hospital, where I found out I had gonorrhea. This was the first time I became aware of the sexually transmitted disease, which I had gotten from Steve's friend. I had to tell him. I was not impressed that Steve's friend knew he had gonorrhea and waited until his friends had had sex with me before he had his turn so that he did not give it to his friends. I broke up with Steve but he was not happy about it as we really liked each other, so we agreed to a six-month break.

I was seventeen and bored with office work and college. I went into the city centre for the second time by myself. The first time I had gone to the city centre was with my mother as she had to accompany me to an agency that provided film extras so I could sign up. She was not keen on me doing this as she said it was not a job that was to the glory of God. The agency took a photo of me to put in their book for clients to choose from.

This time I wanted to find a new job, and I got a job in the biggest and busiest boutique in the city centre, Chelsea Girls (this boutique does not exist anymore). They paid me five pounds fifty pence a week. This was big money for me, plus I got a discount on clothes. And I had no intention of giving my mother my pay packet anymore, but I did give her housekeeping money every week.

Chelsea Girls was every young girl's dream shop. It had all the latest fashions at affordable prices.

My life was moving on, and I met new friends. Sharon, a beautiful, sexy black girl, became my soul sister and my best friend. Sharon's best friend was Layla, a white girl. They had gone to school together. Layla's father was the governor of a prison. Layla wanted to go out with a black boy and used self-tanner as she wanted to be brown, and Anne was another white girl who was just fun to be around. We all wore afro wigs, tall platform boots in bright metallic colours, and miniskirts. We used to sing on the shop floor just for fun, pretending we were Diana Ross and the Supremes. Of course Sharon was Diana

Ross. Sharon was a great actress and entertainer.

Chelsea Girls was packed with young shoppers every day. On Saturdays, you could hardly move. Sharon worked part-time as she was training to be a nurse. We partied at the nightclubs in the city centre but my parents were even harder on me to get home by ten. I did all kinds of things to get into the house. I left the kitchen window partly unlocked, but making sure it looked locked. Then I had to climb over the neighbours' wall with their dogs barking. I tried not to make any noise because I knew our dog, Tessa, would alert my parents. Once I got my dress stuck on the wall and fell very hard on the lawn. One night as I climbed through the kitchen window in the dark, I fell into my father's arms. He just shook his head. And when the window did not work anymore, I left blankets in the adjoining passageway of our neighbours' back door. But as the winter got cold, I could not sleep there, so I used the neighbours' wall and slept in the doghouse with Tessa. She had a big doghouse with a big armchair inside, so I put all the extra blankets in there. Tessa was happy to share with me.

I did not stay at Chelsea Girls for too long as Layla found a new boutique in the shopping centre in front of the escalators that led down into the train station. The boutique was called Bambers (it also is no more). They sold designer clothes by Ossie Clark and Mary Quant. Dresses cost up to twenty-five pounds.

The manager and deputy manager were two beautiful white women who were best friends and enjoyed the good life. They were young at heart and turned a blind eye to whatever we did as they were doing the same. They would wear clothes from the shop and then dry-clean them and put them back on the rack.

A new black British band had become the hottest group in the country. They had a number-one hit record on the chart. They were on television and had played at the army camp where my eldest sister was stationed. They met my sister as she was the only black woman at the time on the base of the Women's Royal Air Force (WRAF), where she was a nurse. They even did a write-up with a picture of her in the newspaper. My mother was so proud that she framed the cutting, which was the centre picture on her wall till the day she died.

The band was playing at the swimming bath's function room one street away from my family home. I got four tickets, and what a night! After the band performed, I went up to talk to them and told them that they had met my sister at the WRAF base. They invited us to come with them to their next gig. From then on, after work, Sharon, Layla, Anne, and I would get on the train and meet the band wherever they were playing. They normally would not go onstage till ten or eleven, so the club would lay on food and drinks in the dressing room. Sharon paired off with the lead singer, and the rest of us paired off with the other members. One white boy played with the band, but he never got involved with any of us.

Anne got pregnant by some other boyfriend and went off to another city to live. We never saw her again. The rest of us still partied with the band all night. Then we got the train straight to work in the morning. One night I had partied very hard and was still quite drunk as I got off the train in the morning. I knew I was ready to throw up. I got to the top of the escalators and saw that the manager was just pushing up the shutters of the shop. I could not hold it anymore and was sick all over the front of the shop. I spent all day on the toilet being sick and sleeping it off. That's how good the managers were. By the evening, I was back on the town partying.

Sharon and the lead singer became very close and spent lots of free time together when he was not out playing gigs. He asked her to settle, but she declined. I can't remember what happened to bring that relationship to an end.

On Saturdays we used to make the shop exciting. We played music and took all the mannequins out of the shop window, then got into the shop window and danced. While the men watched us dance, their partners came into the shop to look at the clothes. Layla was our best salesperson. She had plenty of black friends she could get to come to the shop on Saturdays. While we were dancing, she would be selling. Layla always made sure there was something in it for her.

Every Saturday this handsome black man with the most amazing green eyes came by with his girlfriend. She always came into the shop to look, and he always stayed outside. He and I just had a connection. I liked him very much, and I knew he liked me just as much. I looked forward to seeing him every Saturday. My heart was very open to him, and he would show up in my dreams.

Me and my friends' party habits were to party uptown in the best white nightclubs. When they closed early, we would go to our black neighbourhood nightclubs that were packed and stayed open till late. Then when the club closed, we would find a house party, called *shubin*, and dance close in the dark with some stranger. We called this "dry sex".

By this time, I was going to Sharon's house as it was easier, and we only had to pay for one taxi. Or more often, Sharon found a man with a car to take us home. It was better for us to stick together. I hardly went home. Sharon lived with her mother and her mother's partner. The times when I did go home, Sharon came with me and stayed in the room with me and my younger sister.

I started dating Vince, a very handsome black boy. Sharon was dating Edwin, who was the top man around the black area. We had our own black Hollywood and a who's who that set the pace with regards to fashion, money, and entertainment value. During this period, Bob Marley and the Wailers were new on the scene, and Vince and I followed them to all the clubs where they played. Vince and I dated for around three months, but then he wanted to go back to his ex-girlfriend.

Even though I was having plenty of sex, I was not really enjoying it, as in having an orgasm. And I knew that was why I was having plenty of sex. I was searching for the orgasms that I used to have.

Watching me dance in the shop window on a Saturday was a short black man whose nose looked as if it had been chopped off and then stuck back on. He approached me and asked me to go out with him for dinner. It took more than one ask, but as I was getting bored with not having a steady man, I went to dinner with him. After we'd eaten, he asked me to go to his house, but I said no. Then I started telling him about the glam pictures I had had taken. For some reason, I was carrying them around with me, so I showed them to him to whet his appetite. He said he would pay me twenty-five pounds for one. I agreed, but he said I would have to go home with him to get the money. Of course, I knew this was how he was going to bring me around to having sex with him. I was happy to play the game. With twenty-five pounds at the end, it couldn't be bad.

When I got to his house, I discovered that he lived in one room. I lay on his bed, not really caring what he did to me. And, boy, I went to heaven—and with twenty-five pounds in my pocket. That was the life I enjoyed. I would see him every week, but I would never go to his house until he got me what I wanted in money or shopping. I kept him as my secret stash.

Sharon's mom and her partner went to Jamaica for three weeks, and while they were gone, Sharon and I had a party that went on for a week. There was lots of sex and drinking. The house was full of people we did not know. Sharon and Edwin stayed home all day having sex; she did not go to work. I went to work but could not wait to get back as the party would start all over again. Sharon was Edwin's number-one special girl whom he spent his money on.

There were a few guys in Edwin's group of friends whom I liked. I had a quick thing with one of them, but he was a very quiet young man. He left the group and went off to the United States. I never saw him again. There was Leon, the most eligible and handsome one. He was busy making money the right way. We checked each other out but somehow never did anything about it at that time. Years later, though, he played a big part in my life.

Then, just before Sharon's mother came back from

Jamaica, I saw *him* one night at the black club. He looked just like the handsome guy with green eyes who watched me dance in the shop window on Saturdays. I had to find a way to talk to him. I never smoked, but that night I decided I would smoke. He was smoking, so I went up to him and asked him for a light. Then I asked him if he came to the club often as I had not seen him there before.

He told me his name was Barry and asked me for a dance. Though I did not realise it at the time, I fell in love with him there and then. Barry was at the club with his friend Stewart, who tried to pair up with Sharon, but he was not her type. Barry really liked Sharon more than he liked me. He and Stewart gave us a lift home, and the next night, Barry went to Sharon's house to visit. I asked him if he would prefer to go out with Sharon, but he quickly realised that he did not have enough confidence to deal with Sharon's strong personality. When he found that Sharon was not interested in him, his attention came back to me.

Barry and I spent time together. I was in love with him without knowing it. I continued to go to the club with Barry and Stewart, while Sharon was spending more time with Edwin. They would leave the club and go to other parties, and I would stay with Barry and Stewart.

After the club, we went to what Barry and Stewart told me was Stewart's house. Little did I know it was not Stewart's house but Barry's house. Barry and I used the spare room to have sex, and Stewart used what I know now as Barry's daughter's room to have sex with the girl he was with. Barry told me that Stewart's wife worked nights and weekends. I did not know he was talking about his own wife. Barry was eight years older than me. At seventeen, I was strong and brave, but also naive. He and I always left the house by six in the morning. They say love is blind, and I was truly blinded by and naive about this love. There were certainly plenty of clues.

Barry was into the Black Power movement that was progressing during this period. I never knew about black history or slavery. When I bragged to Barry about how many white men I had been out with, he gave me the black history lesson. I started feeling bad, knowing all the white men I had been with.

And true to his word, Steve turned up during this period to see if I had forgiven him. He wanted to start our relationship over. My life would have taken a different direction if Barry had not shown up in my life.

There was a new excitement in the black community. An American company launched a line of skincare products and cosmetics called Holiday Magic. It had a multilevel marketing plan, and black people, believing that they all could get rich from the scheme, remortgaged their homes for it. It was a beautiful product, and Stewart got me to work with it. I don't know what went wrong, but the plan did not work, the company went bust, and so many people lost their houses.

Chapter 7
My Dream Job

Life was changing again. Layla was in love with a black man. Having become pregnant by him, she moved away. Sharon's training as a nurse was finished so she was focusing on her job, and the boutique Bambers was going to close, so I had to find another job. Since I had started to work in the city centre, I had always had my eyes on working as a beauty consultant, but I knew they were not going to employ me as black women did not get those jobs. Instead I applied for a job in one of the city's biggest flagship department stores. The store also had a pharmacy in the basement with a baby's section selling prams, cots, baby clothes, and everything else related to babies. On the ground floor were the cosmetics, perfumery, and toiletries. Glasses, pens, cards, writing paper, and small gifts for men and women were on the first floor. I got a job with the chemist, taking in and giving out prescriptions and selling over-the-counter medicine. The uniform in that department was a white lab coat. The pharmacist who managed the chemist department was Mr Well. He was a caring man, an angel in human form. He was very supportive towards me.

I expressed my desire to be transferred to the beauty department on the ground floor as then I would stand a better chance of getting a job as a beauty consultant.

When a position came up, Mr Well spoke on my
behalf with Mrs Parks, who was the head buyer
and manager of the beauty department. She agreed
that when a position became available for a general
assistant, I could transfer to that department.

Both of them were true to their word. When a
position became available, I was transferred to the
beauty department. During this period, the total
number of black workers in the store, including me,
was seven: two in the pharmacies, two salesgirls on
the first floor, an electrician, the general handyman,
and one working at the store's own brand Number
Seventeen Cosmetics. The branch manager was a hard
white man. He was not a people person but knew
how to maintain an institutionalised establishment.
He was not too keen on the black staff.

I settled down quickly and was loving the
experience. Soon another black salesgirl joined us on
the ground floor. I was able to work at all the cosmetic
counters as relief during the consultants' breaks or
days off.

I had been learning to drive for some six months
before I met Barry. He would allow me to drive his
car, giving me extra lessons. We stopped going to
what I was told was Stewart's house and had sex
in Barry's car down Lovers' Lane. This was a very
popular location that was used by people to park
their cars and have sex. I soon learned many things
about Barry. He liked drinking and gambling, but
I did not understand that these behaviours were a
problem for him. I had no experience with gambling
or drinking. I had no idea about addictions, about
their signs and behaviours, or that doing these things
could destroy one's life and the people who love and

support that person.

I innocently told Barry that I had money saved up for me by my father, who had opened a bank account in his and my names, adding that when my mother took my pay packet from me, she gave it all to my father to save. Barry pressured me to get my dad to take his name off my account. After I did so and got access to my account, he pressured me to take the money out and give it to him. He wanted to place a bet with all my money on a horse that he was 100 per cent sure would win and give us a return of five hundred pounds. I believed him and gave him the entire amount, sixty-seven pounds, to place on this sure-winning horse. It lost, and I never got a penny back from the bet. Then one day Barry did back a winning horse and won five hundred pounds. He got me to open a bank account and deposit this five hundred pounds. This was supposed to be to make good on my money he had lost. But slowly, he chipped away at the balance, pressuring me to give him small amounts of the money until it was all gone. This was all lost to gambling.

Then one busy afternoon at work, I was on the cash register, serving customers. Two black women came up to me. One was very big and tall; the other was short and fat. The short one said to me, "I hear you're going out with my husband. We are going to wait for you outside the shop to beat you." I looked at them very strangely as I knew that I was not going out with anyone's husband, so I asked her what her husband's name was. She told me his name was Benny, and I told her my boyfriend's name was Barry, so it could not be her husband. She accepted what I said and left, but I was still uncomfortable. In my gut I did not like the feeling I was experiencing. So when I saw Barry that night, I told him what had happened. He just laughed and said it was a madwoman.

I am not sure how long this was after the woman had accused me of going out with her husband, but I was on my way home from work early one afternoon, and as I approached the bus stop, who did I see already on the bus? The woman who had accused me of going out with her husband. And sitting beside her was Barry. My heart fell out of my chest. But I kept cool and pretended that I did not recognise him or her. I held my head high, got on the bus, paid, walked past them, and went to the back of the bus. I sat on the opposite side to them so I could get a full view of both of them without having to move my head or eyes too much. Of course, once he caught sight of me, he gave all his attention to his wife. It was the longest bus ride of my life. When they got off the bus, I looked straight ahead, using my peripheral vision to see where they were going. I was numb and devastated. I still don't know how I managed to carry myself home because my heart was beating outside my chest.

When Barry called me that evening, I was very broken, but I did agree to see him. His story was that he did not love his wife. They had gone to the same school, and he had gotten her pregnant. He married her for the child's sake, but they hadn't gotten on from the day they were married. He threw her wedding ring away a few weeks after they were married as he realised it was a mistake. He said all kinds of unkind things about his wife. He confessed that the house we had gone to for sex when we first met was not Stewart's house, but his. His wife was the one who worked nights and weekends. He also confessed that he had given me a wrong name. He was Benny, not Barry. He claimed he had lied about his name because he always wanted to be called Barry as he never liked the name Benny.

I decided to break off the relationship with him there and then. For the next six months, I dated a very handsome young man named Billy, who was very popular around town.

I was working very hard towards becoming a beauty consultant, and I became very useful to Mrs Parks. She liked an occasional drink during the day. She was a brilliant buyer, and she knew I was very spunky and did not like rules. So when she ran out of her gin, she would come up to me and put some money in my hands, and I would slip out of the shop and buy her a bottle of gin, which I put in her special place. In return, she put my name forward for all the open positions for a beauty consultant. She coached me on what to say and always voted for me to have the position. But the branch manager never wanted me to have such a prestigious position, so he always voted against me.

A position became available with a company called Lentheric, Morny, and Cyclax. This company's supervisor, who used to be an air hostess, was very happy for me to get the position. So, with her vote and Mrs Parks's vote, I landed the perfect job with one of the biggest and best-known concession companies with branded products that had the royal seal of approval. Cyclax was the skincare and make-up brand. Morny was a luxury bath products line. Both had the royal seal of approval. Lentheric produced well-known perfumes such as Tweed,

Tramp, Musk, Amber, and Panache.

This was what I had been dreaming of—a position as a beauty consultant. I had gotten my dream job. And as one of the first black beauty consultants, I believed this was a milestone for all black women. My wages went up to eight pounds with commission based on my sales. I received free products and beautiful free uniforms. I still got my discount on anything I bought in the store. My life was on the upswing and I was in the big leagues.

I was a natural at this job, and I increased my wages by making big commission sales. I learned everything about buying and selling, bookkeeping, taking inventory, and writing reports with the support of the best buyer, Mrs Parks, who taught me so much. My supervisor was great, and the company was very impressed with me as their sales had skyrocketed. The only fly in my ointment was the branch manager. He was racist and had voted against me having the job. He tried to intimidate me every opportunity he had, but my sales spoke volumes within the branch and within the company on a national level.

I was dating a great-looking, sexy guy, making top money in a fabulous job, and I was back partying with my soul sister Sharon. I was on top and could have had any man I wanted. I broke up with Billy to date some other good-looking guy just because I wanted to and could get anything I wanted. I was eighteen and my parents had given up trying to control me.

After six months had passed, my heart was crying silently for something that it was missing. Then one day I received a phone call from Benny, my dream man, the man who had my heart. He said, "I miss you. I love you." He said all the right things to me, things a young, naive, emotional girl wanted to hear. I justified it all to myself even though I knew it was wrong, but in my mind, I loved him already. If it was wrong, I thought, then my heart would never be loving him and missing him the way it was. At that moment in my life, there was no other man for me. The love I was feeling for this man was crazy. I wanted to be the blood that ran through his veins, to be inside him so we would be inseparable. I was on fire for him. If he were to tell me to jump, I would ask, "How high?" No one and nothing else mattered but being with this man.

I could not wait to see him every night. We would drive to Lovers' Lane and I got a very warm blanket that we left in the back of his car. We used it to keep us warm and covered up while we made love in the back seat. I bought four-packs of beer and snacks for him. At the weekend, we would go to the pub and then on to a nightclub to dance. But sometimes, before we got to the nightclub, we would eat at a Chinese restaurant that was across the road from the pub. And I paid for all of this. He never had any money, even though he had a good job as a forklift driver working for a well-known company.

As the relationship developed, there were warning signs that I should run from Benny. He drank a lot and became defensive and angry. But my love for this man was full of compassion. Then he showed me that he had a violent side to him. He was driving me home from Lovers' Lane. I can't remember what set him off, but a few yards from my street, he reached over, opened the car door on my side, and tried to push me out of his car while it was moving. Only

God saved me from falling out of the car. This should have been the biggest sign for me to walk away from Benny, but I stayed in the name of love, giving him the go-ahead to abuse me. As he got comfortable in the relationship, he hurled verbal abuse at me. I never knew people behaved like that. I just wanted my dream to be as perfect as my love for him.

One night when the doorbell rang, I was at home with only my younger sister and brother. It was an unusual night for my parents to be out, but luckily they had gone to an important church meeting. When I answered the door, I saw two women standing there. I recognised one as Benny's wife. The other woman was older, and I found out she was her mother. They asked to see my parents. When I told them that my parents were not at home, the women did not believe me. They started calling out and making noise. My younger brother came to the door and told them get lost, saying that if they didn't, he would smash up their car, and if they came back, he would find them. They never came back again.

The black community was not very big, and everyone knew someone who knew you. I was invited to a friend's wedding reception. Benny's wife also knew this friend, so she and Benny were also attending. Benny told me that she had gone out shopping, trying to find a knockout outfit to compete with me.

Neither of us backed down about going to the wedding reception. She had put on quite a bit of weight But I was young, fit, sexy, and beautiful. And I had no understanding of men. We were both giving it our all. Pam was also a friend of the bride, and she attended the reception with me. Even though Benny did not acknowledge me at the reception, I made him feel jealous because I flirted with other men. There was nothing he could do to claim me as his woman.

I was spending more time with Benny and not seeing Sharon as much. My social life was the pub and Lovers' Lane. On Saturdays, I would go to Marks & Spencer to get Benny a nice jumper or shirt as his clothes were not the best.

One night Benny and I met up in the pub with one of his best friends, who was also married and having an affair. As we left the pub to go across the road to the Chinese restaurant, it started to rain. Benny's friend and his girlfriend were walking ahead of us. I got my umbrella out as the rain was falling heavily. Benny took my umbrella from me, ran after his friend's girlfriend, and covered her head with my umbrella, leaving me to walk in the rain. The worst thing was that they were almost at the restaurant door when he approached them with the umbrella. I was soaked and upset, and my mood did not please him. He kept kicking me under the table. He was winding me up.

At the end of the meal, the other couple went to their car. Benny and I planned to meet them at the nightclub. Benny's car was parked down a very dark side road with only factory buildings and no streetlights. Big potholes in the street were filled with water. As we got to the car, out of the blue, Benny took the umbrella from me and started to beat me with it. The umbrella broke, and the wires were cutting me everywhere. I came to my senses and started to fight back, kicking, digging my fingers into his face, and biting into his arms. We fell into a pothole. I bit him hard, and he let me go. I managed to get up before he did and ran towards my home. I had to pass the closed shopping centre and run across the empty car park; it was the only way for me to get home. He managed to catch up with me in the car park and he got out of his car and attacked me. I had to forget I loved this man and put up a fight as there was not a soul in sight and no car passing—just me and God and this angry man. I bit him in his chest as I started pulling the new jumper I had bought him over his head. While it was stuck over his head, I ran. I had two roads to choose from to get to my house, one of which would have brought me close to the street I lived on. I would have to pass the general hospital and could have gone in there for help, but at the time, I never thought about it. And if I had gone down the hospital road, it would have been too open with nowhere to hide. So I chose the road that was not so open. There were houses with alleyways I could hide in.

I saw Benny slowly driving by and turn right on to the main road that led off the street I lived on. He positioned himself outside my house to wait. If I had gone down the hospital street, he would have caught up with me. Thank God I had made the right choice. I was able to sneak into someone's alleyway at the top of my street, from where I could watch him. We both waited. Finally, he got tired of waiting. I saw him drive off slowly. As he got to the bottom of my street and turned left, I bolted to my house.

I did not hear from him for some weeks. I had to hide from my parents as I had cuts and bruises all over me. Thank God my younger sister helped to cover for me.

Of course, when Benny called me, it was all "Sorry,

sorry, sorry." And what did I do? I went back to him.

His drinking got worse. When we went out on a Saturday night, I always ended up having to drive the car, drop him off at his house, and then drive myself home. Then on Sunday, I would pick him up at his house. I started cooking for him on Sundays as everyone from my house went to church and I had the house to myself all day. I would buy him a big steak fit for a king with all the trimmings for his Sunday dinner. We ate together, and it made me feel good.

I started living dangerously. Our spare room downstairs was empty, and we kept mountains of washed clothes on the bed. There was a sofa next to the window. The space between the sofa and the bed made it easy to lie on the floor between them, where no one could see us. As long as we were quiet, we could sleep comfortably and be warm.

My job was going well. I was always number one in sales over the entire country, and I often travelled to meetings in the big city.

By the time I was twenty-one, the age of consent, I was ready to find my own apartment as I was tired of hiding. I started looking for my own flat. I did not tell Benny I was looking to leave home. I decided I wanted to live well away from both our communities, and I wanted to go upmarket and stylish. I did not have to look too long before I was blessed with a brand-new two-bedroom apartment from a housing association. I was the first person to move into the apartments. The workmen were still working on the apartments when I moved in.

Having the right job went a long way to me getting the apartment, which was on a cul-de-sac with trees, beautiful lawns and gardens, and parking. The apartments were in a three-storey building. I was on the first floor with a big balcony, a built-in wardrobe, storage cupboards, and a beautifully fitted kitchen. This was my dream home. My new furniture was retro brown and smoke-glass with an orange patchwork-type sofa and curtains. The living room passage and bedrooms were carpeted. My mother was very kind to give me enough money so I could fit-out the whole apartment with pots and pans, cutlery, and bedding. I bought a front-loading washing machine and a fridge-freezer.

Now I was a big woman with my own front door keys. I spent the first week in my apartment alone. By the second week, Benny asked me for a key. When I came home from work one Monday evening, he was already in my bed, sleeping, as he worked nights. I cooked something quickly, so I would have time to jump into bed with him for an hour. On Friday he had started moving some of his clothes in slowly in black bags. His shift was two to six, and he never came home till Monday evening. I was at home by myself at weekends, so I started going out with my girlfriends. I never saw him out and never asked him any questions. As far as I was concerned, he was living at home with his wife. Little did I know that he had long moved out of the marital home and was living with a woman at the end of the street where he and his wife had their house.

I started having affairs. I picked up where I had left off with the short little black man to whom I had sold my glam photograph. I would meet him in town on my day off, get him to buy some expensive things, and then have orgasmic sex with him. I started having a fling with Leon, who was part of the earlier group of friends I used to go around with. We had always had a little spark for each other. He became the first young, black, handsome millionaire in our community. If I had had any sense at the time, I would have left Benny and settled with Leon. He was keen on a long-term relationship with me, but my heart was so in love with Benny that I could not see my life with anyone but him. Leon married someone else. His young wife always came into the store and lingered around my counter, trying things on and asking about prices. I am sure she must have known about me and Leon and that I, not she, could have been his wife.

A very handsome older white man named Patrick used to come by my counter and buy perfume. Sometimes he just came by to chat me up, so I started seeing him on my days off. He owned a car dealership. He would take me to expensive restaurants, and after we had eaten, he would take me to a beautiful hotel. Patrick would get me to dress up in a nurse's uniform, and then I would take care of him.

Then the strangest thing happened. One day the young man I had been so crazy about who used to watch us dancing on Saturdays in the shop window walked past my counter. He was the spitting image of Benny. He started coming by regularly and would stop to talk to me.

I got my younger sister a Saturday job in the store and I met my soul mother, Karen, who started to work at the store.

One Monday morning I had a half-day off work to attend an appointment. I was on my way to my appointment, and who did I see? Benny, with some woman who was not his wife. He saw me and kept his head straight ahead. His body language said, *don't even come and ask me anything*. It made me think again about how he never spent weekends at my apartment. He said it was too far from his friends, and since he liked to drink, it was better for him to stay over on his regular side of town.

Benny did not come home that Monday night. Nor did he call me. I did not see him for some time. That was a clear message that he did not want me to ask him any questions. I started going through the few clothes that he had at my apartment. I searched through his pockets and found a girl's name and number. Of course, I called the number as I was young and foolish. It was her work number. She knew about me and told me that Benny had left his wife a long time ago. He was now living with her, and she was pregnant. This was the woman I had seen him with on the way to my appointment. I was alone in my beautiful apartment and wanted to kill myself. I kept taking aspirin, but it just put me in a deep sleep. I woke up alive and pulled myself together. What I was doing did not make sense as I was out there doing the same thing he was doing. But jealousy has an ugly face.

Benny finally came home and stayed over on Friday night. On Saturday, when he was leaving to go out, I got into the back of his car and lay on the floor. I wanted to see where he was going, but he realised I was in the car. We argued and got into a fight. He drove back to the apartment, and we went indoors. We wrestled like two big bears. All my new furniture was broken in the process and I got the biggest black eye. After the fight, Benny went out and bought the biggest piece of steak to put on it. Then he cooked the steak. It was a miracle my eldest sister did not see me as she and her husband had moved into the block of apartments next to mine.

As time went by, Benny started to live with me more, but I never saw any of his wages. It was then that I realised the scale of his gambling. I had to take care of everything. I even gave him money to pay for his daughter's maintenance as his wife still blamed me for the break-up of their marriage. I got brave and asked him about the pregnant girl he was living with, and he told me that she had had a miscarriage. Years later, I found out he had lied. He never would admit that he had another child with her.

I never met any of Benny's family. I knew he had two brothers and one sister. His mother and father were both Jamaican-Indian. One day he asked me to prepare some food as he had invited his younger brother over. When he arrived, to our surprise, he was the young man who had watched me dance in the window and was coming by my counter to say hello. He was the man I really wanted to fall in love with. We both were in shock and did not know what to do, but we got through the shock.

By this time, I was developing a tough skin for love as it was not the fairy tale that I had dreamed of. Sharon went off to live in Switzerland as she had met and married a Swiss man.

Benny's brother and I kept showing up at the same house parties. We danced close all night, and soon we had built up a strong energy. We wanted to see if there was something there, so I went to his apartment one night, but for some reason, we could not have sex. We wanted to, but we just talked, cuddled, and got to know each other. I knew that if we had had the right chance, we would have been perfect for each other. He was very handsome with green eyes and the softest, kindest heart. We still are the greatest of friends with happy memories.

My eldest sister went to Dubai to work. My brother-in-law was friendly with Benny and we all started to play squash on a Sunday, along with my second-eldest brother and his wife. My brother got so good that he started playing in the league. My sister-in-law and I played together, and we got good at the game. After work, my sister-in-law and I would coach a few of the black girls I worked with to play squash. My sister-in-law knew the girls from when she had worked with me for a few Christmases. On Saturday evenings, I would cook. Benny, my second-eldest brother and his wife, my brother-in-law, and Benny's best friend, Stewart, all came to my apartment to play dominoes, eat, drink, and play music.

I was still seeing the handsome white man. He was encouraging me to find a shop, saying he would put up the money for me to sell products aimed at black people. These would include hair products and cosmetics, and there would be a section for hairdressing. I really wanted to do this, but how was I going to explain this man's existence to Benny? The only things he wanted from life were to gamble and to drink. I was young and had no idea how to handle this. We were arguing much more over anything. One day we were arguing in the kitchen, and he opened the kitchen cupboard and started to smash plates, cups, and glasses. It was a war zone with broken glass everywhere, dangerously flying through the air. How neither of us were not hurt was a miracle. Both of us should have been stabbed by flying glass. As he kept smashing, I began to see red, and all the love I had for him left my heart. I pulled my right hand back into a tight fist, and with all the strength I had in me, I connected my fist fully with his face. Like in a slow-motion movie, blood sprayed everywhere from his nose and mouth. His head went from side to side. By the time he caught his balance and came round, he was in shock. His lips were cut and swollen. I had put a stop to his madness.

We both were in shock. For the next two weeks, he could not leave the apartment. I had to move his car and stop everyone from coming to the apartment. My brother-in-law knew something was up, but when he came over, Benny would hide in the wardrobe. In my heart I was already shutting down from this love. From the day my fist connected with Benny's face, I knew I wanted a way out of the relationship.

Chapter 8
The Birth of My Son

When I was growing up in England from the sixties to the eighties, when it snowed, it snowed. And it was cold. The snow was always heavy and deep. It was now 1978, and I had no thoughts of having a baby. I had been on the pill since I was sixteen, but there was talk about long-term use of the pill causing blood clots. It was advised that women take a break, so I decided to take a break from the pill. I was also making plans to give up my apartment and go back home, find a new job, and make a fresh start as a way out of the relationship with Benny. It was not going to work, and I did not want to try anymore, so I came off the pill and never gave a thought to the notion that I could get pregnant very quickly after having used the pill for many years. In my mind, it would take some time to get the pill out of my system.

My plan was to go into retail management as this was my best option because of my previous experience before I worked for Lentheric, Morny, and Cyclax. Combining this with my experience as a beauty consultant, I knew I could secure a good job. Over the years that I had worked for Lentheric, Morny, and Cyclax, I had several supervisors. One was a racist blonde woman. She was not happy with me winning all the sales competitions, so she changed the criteria to percentage sales. This meant I would have to sell thousands more than I was selling to win anything. She employed a blonde, white girl, Jill, to work part-time with me. But what she didn't know was that Jill had a black lover and all her friends were black. I was also good friends with another white girl, April, who was the beauty consultant for a company called Almay. Her counter was next to mine. She also had a young assistant working with her. The four of us were close. We talked about our love lives, as women do.

Things were changing in the beauty department. The manager of the store was having an affair with Mrs Parks' assistant buyer, Jeana. She was engaged but wanted the position as head buyer more than she wanted to get married. Jeana allowed the manager to use her and was making things difficult for Mrs Parks. As we prepared for Christmas 1978, April's assistant found out she was pregnant.

It was turning out to be one of those bad winters, very cold with heavy snow. The Christmas period was the busiest time of the year for the store and the most demanding for all consultants. There was so much pressure to make big sales to meet targets. I started work earlier and finished later to meet the Christmas demand.

My second-eldest brother and his wife invited Benny and me to have Christmas dinner with them. Christmas Eve was always a very busy time with the madness of last-minute shoppers. By the time the shop closed, I was totally exhausted. The snow had built up quite deep and was still falling heavily. Benny was supposed to pick me up. I waited about an hour for him, and as there was no way of calling him to find out what he was doing, I decided to take the bus. But the snow was so bad that the bus could not go all the way, so I had to walk quite a distance to get home. When I got home, I was cold and wet, and felt as if I was coming down with something. I never heard from Benny, and with the roads out of action, it was the perfect excuse for him. He never even called me to say he was not going to be home. There was no way my brother could have driven to get me, so I spent Christmas alone in bed with the flu.

I had to take time off work after the Christmas period as I was not recovering from the flu. I just could not shake it off. By New Year, I still hadn't heard from Benny, so I ended up also seeing in the new year in alone.

During the Christmas and New Year's celebrations, I had plenty of time to reflect and was ready to put my plans into action. The relationship with Benny was not what I had dreamed about; there was no point to it. The love I had for him was fading fast. I just wanted to get as far away from him as I could.

When I returned to work in the new year, I saw a great job opening as the manager of a new clothing boutique. I arranged for an interview during my lunch break, but on that day, I was feeling very sick. The girls I worked with said it sounded more like I was pregnant. I compared how I was feeling with April's pregnant assistant. They suggested that I get a pregnancy test at the women's clinic located a few minutes from the store rather than go to the interview, and that's what I did.

In that hour lunch break, my life changed. I was pregnant. I sat in the room with the nurse who had given me the result and felt as if I were in a strange bubble, a fish out of water. I was in another world. I could not go home pregnant as my dad would not put up with it; having a child out of wedlock was against his religion. He was not pleased with me having left home and living with a man without being married. I believe my parents did not know that Benny was a married man.

But I wanted my baby. I just did not want the father. All the love I had for Benny was now growing inside me. I never thought about my heart, whether it could cope. I started talking to my baby. One night I had a dream that he was a boy.

When Benny eventually turned up, I told him I was pregnant. He was not happy. What I really wanted was for him to leave as I did not feel any love for him. Then the strangest thing happened, he fell in love with me deeply, and I fell out of love with him. My son was my world. I asked him to be a good boy in my tummy and to help me to carry him safely before delivering him into the world.

The changes in Benny were unbelievable. He went to work and then came home. He never went out with his friends. He picked me up from work, took me shopping, and did all the cooking as I could not stand the smell of meat cooking. He did not gamble. Benny gave me his wages on each Friday and took only enough money for his weekly petrol and beer. I didn't know what had come over this man.

My parents were planning to return to Jamaica for good. My dad had retired and was waiting for my mother to retire. Then they would sell their house and return home to Jamaica. My lover Patrick secretly supported me financially during my pregnancy. At some point during my pregnancy, he told me he had divorced his wife and had sold his car dealership and was going to live in the United States. When he got settled, he said he would write me. To this day, I have never heard from him.

My pregnancy was a good one, though the time went slow. I did not suffer any medical problems. My baby boy and I were working together, and I had plenty of support from the girls at work. My assistant, Jill, was the best. She kept me informed of whatever my supervisor was saying to her. The supervisor thought since she and Jill were both white, Jill would be loyal to her and not to me. My supervisor was trying to get rid of me; she hoped I would not come back to work after my maternity leave. She was hoping that Jill would help her work on me and had promised her my job. So before I went on maternity leave, I knew she was trying to get rid of me. By this time, the store manager and Jeana had managed to get Mrs Parks to resign. So there was no more Mrs Parks in my corner. She died a year or so later, and it was kept a big secret.

In the middle of summer, I went on my maternity leave. It was one of those very hot English summers. My parents had gone home to Jamaica for six weeks. This was the first time my father had returned to Jamaica since leaving when I was five years old. It was also the first time my mother had returned since she had left Jamaica to join my father. They planned to come back before my due date. I was their first daughter to have a child, and not knowing how my heart would cope, my mother wanted to be there for me in the weeks up to my giving birth. My two eldest nieces came to stay with me as this was during their summer holiday. They would be with me all the time to raise any alarm.

I went into slow labour on a Monday. During this time, I could not sleep or sit still. I cleaned every window and mopped the kitchen floor over and over. By Friday night, I knew I was ready, and at six on Saturday morning, I was ready to call the ambulance, but I waited until nine, counting the contractions.

Benny went with me to the hospital but soon disappeared. I spent most of the day using gas and air and sleeping. My eldest sister was back from Saudi and was working at the hospital where I was having my baby. Since she was on duty that day, she popped in and out to see me. I made it quite clear to the delivery team that under no circumstances were they to use forceps on my baby's head.

Apart from my sister popping in and out and the delivery team, I was alone at 6.20 p.m., when I gave birth to my son. He was perfect in every way. In those days, new mothers had to stay in hospital for a week. I got friendly with the young black woman who had given birth to her baby girl a half an hour before me. We're still in contact. She's also friends with my family and circle of friends.

When Benny finally turned up on Sunday, he was drunk. According to him, he had been celebrating.

My friend Karen and a few other girls from work came to visit me and my son. The joy I was feeling and the love for my son was more than I could express. He was a small baby, which was helpful to me. He did a lot of sleeping and not much drinking. He wasn't a crier. My baby boy was cute and handsome.

It was good to get home with my beautiful son. Benny was attentive and enjoyed his son. I had no problem with motherhood. It was easy for me, and I loved every moment.

I had a beautiful budgie that I called Kaya. I got the name from Bob Marley's album cover. I used to let her fly around the apartment. Kaya flew onto the balcony, sat at the open window, and never flew away. I taught her to talk and say, "Pretty, pretty, pretty Kaya," and "Who is a pretty, pretty Kaya?" She was very attentive to me. But when I arrived home with my son, Kaya got jealous and would attack my son or me. I had to lock her up in her cage. As my son grew, I allowed Kaya out of her cage. Then my son and Kaya developed a special relationship.

My son was born with a slight heart murmur but soon grew out of it. He did suffer from infantile eczema. He had it so bad that when you picked him up, all his skin would come off on you. He had to be hospitalised for weeks and was bandaged from head to toe. Only his eyes, nose, and mouth were left out. I was challenged to use my natural gifts I did not realise I had for skincare to get my son through his eczema.

I had planned to take seven months for maternity leave, but by November, three months into my maternity leave, Jill called me and advised me to return to work as my supervisor was planning to find a way to get rid of me. Jill did not want my job and was planning to give the supervisor her notice. Christmas season was getting ready to start. Before I had gone on maternity leave, I had placed the Christmas order. So I decided to return to work as it was in my interests to get the big Christmas commission from the Christmas sales. Babysitting was not a problem. Benny worked nights, and he slept when our son slept. If he needed any help, my eldest sister and her husband were next door. My brother-in-law was very helpful. Our son was living at both apartments and was totally loved.

My assistant, Jill, did leave as she did not want to deal with the politics my supervisor was creating with the support of the store manager. Between the two of them, they did little things to irritate me, but I did not take the bait. Instead, I printed some cards and gave them out to black women, inviting them and their friends to a make-up party. I had found a company in the big city called Shades of Black. It was owned by a Jewish man with a black girl as his assistant. They imported black make-up from the United States. I purchased make-up from them, and ran make-up parties for the ladies I had given my card to. I also did makeovers and was making good money. My idea was to make enough money to open my own shop. That idea, inspired by Patrick, was still very attractive and growing in my head.

My sales were big enough for Shades of Black to notice that I was outselling them. Their plans were to retail the cosmetics in one of the other big department stores in the city where I worked The owner approached me with a plan to have two weeks of promotion in the store. The lady whose brand of cosmetics he was selling would come from the United States and do makeovers and demonstrations for black women. I would be part of the team helping her. He asked me to do all the radio promotions leading up to the demonstrations. Then the consultant position in that store would be mine, he said, after the two weeks of demonstrations. This was an opportunity for me to move on but still have a dream job, so I accepted the offer without a written contract. My plan was to take a one-week holiday from my job to work on the first week of promotions and then go back to my job and hand in my notice to take up my position as consultant for Shades of Black.

I was excited by the new prospect of another dream job. I was ready for the change as the pressure was on me from my supervisor and the store manager. I was offered redundancy, and I refused.

I was young and had no experience in handling the challenges I currently was facing. I did not understand the importance of a contract and had never even read the contract I had signed when I got my dream job with Lentheric, Morny, Cyclax. Unbeknown to me, that contract stated that I was not allowed to work with any other company or promote any other products that were in direct competition with the company's products that I was representing.

Chapter 9
My Trendsetting Jobs

So with the excitement of a new job, doing my first interview on BBC Radio, and my first make-up demonstration, I felt invincible. Of course, I was sharing my exciting news with April, my white girlfriend who worked for Almay Cosmetics. I shared everything with her as I thought she was a trusted friend.

I booked off a week's holiday to work on the Shades of Black promotion, and on a Monday morning, I kicked off the promotion. I went to BBC Radio to do my first interview promoting the upcoming launch of Shades of Black cosmetics. I enjoyed the interview very much. I was a natural at it. I was about fifteen minutes late getting to work that morning, and when I made my excuse as to why I was late, Jeana confronted me. She had heard me on the radio show that morning. I denied it, but she said she was sure it was me.

I noticed that April was behaving oddly. She had sold me out, and she knew what the supervisors' plans were for me.

As the time for the launch got closer, I could feel the changes in April's behaviour. But I was so excited that I did not realise how dangerous she was. When the day came for the launch the following Monday, I was full of excitement at meeting this glamorous

American black woman who was the owner of Zuri Cosmetics. She was the first black American woman I had ever met. I would see these beautiful black African-American women in the American magazine *Ebony* and wish I could look like them.

By the end of the day, word had spread in the community and the surrounding areas. I had to learn a lot by Tuesday. The local television station came to interview the company's owner, and the crowd got bigger by the day. By Thursday, a black man had joined the team. He seemed to want to take over my position. He worked for a big-brand chocolate company and was not a good make-up artist, but he had a lot of talk.

Black women came from far and wide, buying everything. For the first time, black women had make-up that had been made especially for their skin colour. The store did not have the capacity for the number of black women who came. Some came every day as they waited to get a makeover or to get a chance to try the colours. This was the job I wanted to do every day. My excitement was beyond words.

Then on Friday afternoon, my world collapsed. I don't know how I was spared from having a heart attack. There in the crowd of hundreds of black women, a white woman with pale-blonde hair worked her way to the front and stood there, looking at me. I could not move, breathe, or talk. My supervisor came up to me and said, "Please don't return to work on Monday morning as you're sacked. Check the contract that you signed." Then she walked away. It was as if everything was collapsing in on me. But I was holding on; I had to keep breathing. I had to keep standing. Even with all these people around me, no one knew what had happened. I comforted myself that it was OK. I had a new job starting, and this did not matter.

On Saturday, I asked Shades of Black if I could do the second week of the promotion and was told no. The black man who had joined the team was working, and he brought in a young black woman to join the team. I was still in total shock.

When I read my contract, I found that it did state that I was not allowed to work during my holiday period or part-time in any way that would be in direct competition with Lentheric, Morny, and Cyclax. In my mind, working as a make-up artist for black people was in no way competition for my current job, and I really thought I could argue the case.

I went into the store to see my so-called friend April. She was very sheepish. She held her head down and pretended she was busy. She could not look at me, knowing that I knew she was the one who had sold me out to the store and my supervisor. I got no joy from going to see her.

In the days that followed, I went to the main office to see the head boss of the company. I thought he would stick up for me because, during the years I had worked for the company, I had a good relationship with him, and I had made the company so much money over the eight years. But he was hostile. I just wasted my time and added more pain to my heart. There was no tribunal set-up for discrimination during this period as there is now. And because there was no clear policy against racial discrimination, no one was prepared to take my case on. I had to walk away helpless.

I kept my spirits up knowing I had the job as the

beauty consultant for Shades of Black at the end of the promotion, but there was another big shock in store for me when I called to make arrangements to take up that position. The man told me the job had been given to the young woman who had been introduced by the man who had worked for the chocolate company. The man at Shades of Black did want me to work on a roadshow going around the country, promoting the make-up. It was a nice offer, but it was not what I wanted nor what I had been promised. But with a heavy heart, I did it. The job lasted only three weeks as there were not that many events to go to. At the end of the three weeks, the man did not pay me for the roadshow or demonstration for which I had lost my job. It took months of phone calls to get paid.

I knew getting another job as a beauty consultant was not going to happen. Other department stores or cosmetic concessions were not employing black women.

I was still hurting and had no more fight left in me, so I got a job for six months in the office of an engineering company that made oil seals. I took orders and called former customers for their business. The job was about ten minutes from my house. It was a boring job with boring people. They asked me to stay on for another six months.

My beautiful son was growing fast; he was walking and talking by the time he was one year old. At the weekends, we spent a lot of time going to the park. His father was attentive.

As the office job was coming to an end, I was still bored with it and started looking to move on. I spotted a small advert in the *Jamaican Gleaner*, a black newspaper, that an American company was looking for staff to work with their cosmetics. The job was in another big city. I made the call and got an interview set up for a Saturday. The name of the company was Hollywood Curls Sahara Springs Cosmetics, and my interview was at a hairdressing shop called Timeless Hair and Beauty Salon. Mrs Marley, the owner of Hollywood Curls Sahara Springs Cosmetics, was a very flamboyant black American woman with long hair and long nails. I was asked to bring a model, so I got my sister-in-law to come with me as my model. As part of the interview, I had to do a makeover using the company's products.

I got the job! My first assignment was to work a professional hair and beauty event call Salon Eighties at a big exhibition centre with a big team of hairdressers and other make-up artists. All I had to do was make up mostly young white girls who wanted to try the products. As the colours were for black women, they were very vibrant on white skin.

Ours was the only stand demonstrating make-up, so we were busy. The hairdressers were demonstrating the new wet-look curly perm, the biggest hair product of the eighties. It was not just black women who were using the curly perm; black men used it too.

Hollywood Curls was the leader of the wet-look curly perm for black hair. Not only was Mrs Marley, the owner of this brand, flamboyant, but also with the marketing strategies, she brought a new kind of enthusiasm to black men and women.

Hollywood Curls brought across some of its American workers, and this built a strong, fun team who knew how to draw people to the stands to showcase their products. I was a natural at the job.

The show was for two days. I was booked into the

Holiday Inn in an affluent area. I felt rich, powerful, and happy. It was a dream job, and they paid on time. This was the life!

This was my first time away from my son, and I missed him. The morning after the event, I packed my bags so I could check-out after breakfast. As I walked back to my room to collect my luggage, coming towards me was the tallest black African man, dressed in his traditional outfit. He came right up to me and said, "Good morning." I was in such shock but said good morning back. He asked if I would like to have breakfast with him. I told him I had just finished breakfast, so he suggested I have a coffee while he ate. I don't know what possessed me, but I was intrigued and said yes.

As we talked, he said he was a prince back in his country of Nigeria, but he was also a foreign minister. Our conversation drifted to sex, and he said I should come to his room and stay, going home in the evening instead. I said that I could, but it would cost him a lot of money. He told me to name my price. I said, just for fun, one thousand pounds. I was totally gobsmacked when he said yes. I was in a new league.

With the excitement of one thousand pounds, we went to my room, collected my suitcase and put it in his room, checked out, and went to his room. I asked him to show me the money first, and he opened a briefcase full of money. All I had to do was lie there and think how I was going to spend the money. And that is what I did. But something else was happening while I was thinking about the big money: my body was loving the sex. And I was thinking, *If my friends could see me now with him.* He was no five-minute man—thirty minutes, easy—and we both wanted more and more. I could not get enough. I did not want it to end, and he wanted me to stay the night. And, boy, I wanted to as I'd never had sex like that, one session after another, but I had to think about my son. So with my one thousand pounds, I was back on the train towards home. But the Nigerian Prince would be back in three weeks, when we would spend three days together.

By the time I got home, I had already decided to tell Benny the truth. I really did not care if our relationship ended. Besides, I knew he would be cool with it as he was gambling and drinking again. He could not stop me from doing what I wanted to do to make money as he was putting pressure on me with his addictions.

Sure enough, Prince arrived back in England, and I spent three days with him. He was staying in a beautiful hotel. I went shopping during the day, and in the evening, we went out and ate at very expensive restaurants. I got money for shopping as well as my thousand pounds.

I enjoyed the good life and the good sex, but I was a little bit embarrassed for people to see me with Prince. It was something I had to get used to, but I knew I would never let any of my friends see me with him.

I was offered a full-time job with Hollywood Curls to run the beauty department and promote Sahara Springs Cosmetics. This meant that I had to live in the city during the week. I arranged to stay with my girlfriend Madge, who used to work with me in the store before moving to the city. I would get the train on Monday morning and return home on Saturday evening. My son stayed with my parents during the week as my father had retired.

Promoting Sahara Springs Cosmetics took me to the major cities all over England. I sometimes also had to work in my hometown. The clientele who came to Hollywood Curls Salon were very rich African ladies who carried so much money crumpled up in big handbags that when they opened their bags, the money would jump up. They would take out whatever jumped up, as they only carried fifties, twenties, and tens, and never accepted their change after they had paid. When they tipped you, it was a good day when the fifty-pound bill jumped out. There were days when we had photo shoots and planned small events, big beauty exhibitions, beauty competitions, and fashion shows. There was so much to do organising a lifestyle event that got black people to showcase their creativity, beauty, and networking abilities. This was how we set the trend for one of our biggest achievements: creating *Black Hair and Beauty Magazine*. The magazine would be able to reach many more black women in England.

The job doing make-up for the magazine's first photo shoot was given to me and May, another member of the team. This photo shoot was to be in colour and would be a challenge not just for us but also for the photographer, as magazines in those days were in black and white. The photo shoot was for the front cover and the centre-page spread, and the photographer was not able to guide us as we had no experience to gauge what colour make-up should be used. We never got to see the photographs until we bought the first issue of *Black Hair and Beauty Magazine*. The make-up was so bold that May and I were embarrassed. On reflection, if we were to do this kind of make-up today, we would call it retro.

The black people who had the money in those days were Africans. They brought a great deal of money from Africa so they could spend big in England. They walked around with briefcases full of money. There were even true stories of them forgetting their briefcases of money in the backs of taxis. I had many rich African boyfriends. I partied with this flashy young man about my age. He had a sports car. The champagne nightclub lifestyle described the preference of another of the guys I was seeing.

I was still seeing my African prince. He asked me to marry him in England, to be his second wife, so he could set up a bank account to look after me properly and legally. I was afraid of the word *marriage*. I don't regret not doing it, but it would have been interesting to see what my financial path would look like now had I married him. He just wanted to make life easy for me as that's what princes do for princesses.

Then one day I met the real African love of my life, Craig. My heart just knew. One evening Mrs Marley and I sat by the window in the make-up room upstairs from the hair salon. She was giving me instructions as she was planning to go back to the United States for a few weeks, and I was second in charge not just for the beauty department, but also for the hair salon. We were both looking out the open window, when stepping out of a beautiful mint-green Mercedes was a six-foot tall, beautifully dressed black man with the perfect body. He walked into the salon. After a few minutes, the door of the beauty room opened, and he walked in. Mrs Marley called him by name. My heart pretended it did not like him and I looked away, but his voice was like music to my ears.

I looked out the window as he talked to Mrs Marley. I thought, *This beautiful car looks like him*. When he left, I was already in position at the window to see him look up at me from outside. He smiled, got in his sexy car, and drove away slowly with my heart.

I didn't think about him again. Then a week later, after Mrs Marley had left for the United States, he drove up. I was sitting at the reception desk when he came in and asked me if he could talk with me upstairs in the beauty room. So we went upstairs. He asked me if he could pick me up after work and take me out for something to eat. I said yes. We agreed on a time. Then he asked me if I had eaten lunch. When I said no, he gave me twenty pounds to buy lunch, then left. I did not spend all the money on my lunch. I also bought a nail scissors which I kept for over twenty years. And that's how long, or longer, he remained in my life. In that time, my life journey was guided by my love for Craig, my African love.

True to his word, he picked me up on time for dinner. We went to a famous glass restaurant in a very affluent area. Many famous people were dining there. And who did I see? The lead singer from the band we used to follow! But I did not let him see me.

Craig had two shops selling men's and women's fashions. We were born under the same astrological sign. He had just gotten divorced from his wife, with whom he had two children. He was arrogant and liked to be in control. I was the passive one.

He gave me the address of his shop and asked me to come and see him on Saturday before I returned home for the weekend. I went to see him. Little did I know I was in a game played by a real player. With all the experience I thought I had at twenty-six, my lessons had just begun. He played with women, of which he had many. He got all of us to come to see him at his shop, where we would all meet. He introduced us to each other, knowing we would be jealous of each other. Craig was quite cold and narcissistic, but from the beginning, I was in love with him.

The following week he called me and asked me out, but this time we did not go to dinner, and I was not involved in that decision. He booked a hotel room, and we made love and spent the night together. Over the years that we were together, everything had to be on his terms. The first time of passion is always the best; his body was black, silky, and perfect. I found his arrogance interesting and sexy.

After that night, he fell into his bad habit of keeping me waiting all night to pick me up if we had a date. Sometimes he would not show up, and he would never allow me to ask him any questions. All he would say was that he was busy.

He quickly asked me to move in with him, to leave my home and bring my son to be with him. I was not feeling him as much as I was falling for him. I was not going to move in with him and upset my son's balanced life. Craig was not happy that I had said no. Afterwards, his behaviour changed towards me.

I had planned a birthday party for my son. I had told Mrs Marley about this before she returned to the United States, and she had promised she would be back before I had the week off for his birthday. However, it didn't work out and she didn't get back on time. She gave the manager a message to tell me that if I took the time off, I should not come back to work as she needed someone she could rely on.

One of the young men I used to go nightclubbing

with was one of those rich boys from Gambia. His uncle was opening an InterContinental Hotel and was looking for a beauty therapist to run the spa. He introduced me to his uncle, who was happy to give me the job of setting up the spa. We agreed on a salary. He was getting my contract ready for me to sign when, on our next meeting, he asked me to bring my certificate. I did not have any certificate. The kind of beauty he wanted was more than what I could do. I had to make an excuse that I could not organise a childminder to look after my son, so I had to turn down the job offer. When Mrs Marley gave me no choice about coming back to work if I took my holiday, I was brave enough to take my holiday and gave up the job.

I decided that I needed to go to beauty school to train and become a qualified beauty therapist. Since I was not working, I could go full-time. I found a school not far from where I lived. Luckily for me, the lady who owned the school was the head of the Beauty Therapist Association. In those days, all the beauty schools were private.

Now the problem for me was that to get into beauty school, I needed science and English GCSE qualifications, but I had no qualifications as I had left school in a hurry. Another problem was the fee of five hundred pounds. Despite all the money I was making, I did not have enough to pay the fee. The owner of the school asked me to come and see her. She said that with all the experience I had, she was going to give me a chance and allow me to do the course. She told me not to let myself down and to make sure I passed.

I asked my mother to help me with the finances,

and I was shocked when she said yes. She paid for the whole course. I was very excited, and for the next six months, I let nothing get in my way. It was good to be back home and with my son, though I did miss the big city life. I called Craig at least twice a week, or more if I could, and hoped he had the time to talk to me. I never called Mrs Marley to beg for my job back.

I was on a high as I did well at my training and enjoyed it a lot, though I didn't have many plans for after my training. I came to realise that I was far cleverer than I had known. When I applied myself, it really all came very easily. I had a brilliant teacher.

Just before I finished my training, I had a call from Mrs Marley. She asked if I would come back as they had a Salon Eighties exhibition to do and needed staff. I would be working as a freelancer, so I asked her for the daily rate that I knew the other freelance workers were getting, and I got it. Things came together nicely as it was at the end of my training, and my confidence was boosted. I felt on top of the world as I would now be a professional beauty therapist.

Our work at the show was a big hit, and we won best stand. Lots of the big black American brands followed Hollywood Curls and exhibited at the show. The funniest thing happened as I was on the platform demonstrating. I looked into the crowd of mostly white women, and standing in the crowd was this big, tall black African man in full tribal cloth watching me. It was my African prince, and he was not going away. When I got a chance to go for a break, he and I talked. I didn't know he was going to be in England again and had not seen him since before I had started my beauty therapist training. We arranged to meet later at the private flat he was staying in, not far from the salon. He had gone to the salon and found out that I was working at the exhibition. He had no idea that I had just been reinstated to the job. Actually, he didn't know I had been sacked.

I hung out with him for four days and was glad for the extra money. I had a meeting with Mrs Marley, and she agreed I could have my job back and work as a freelancer.

There was a black distribution company that was growing fast. All the American companies were now looking at England as a place to do business, including this company, Dyke & Dryden. Their marketing manager, Roger, was a young man with a vision. We had met many times on the beauty circuit. It was from his vision that the Afro Hair and Beauty exhibition was born. There were enough black brands to separate from the Salon Eighties. I called Roger and arranged an appointment to see him to discuss how I could contribute to the exhibition. From that day forward, he has guided my career every step of the way.

This was an exciting time for black people to showcase their talents and skills. We could inspire changes and increase confidence in black women's and men's appearance and style. The excitement in the black community was good for me as it allowed me to combine my new skincare and make-up skills.

The Afro Hair and Beauty exhibition lasted for two days. The media coverage was big—radio, television, newspaper, and magazine. Demonstrating mini-facials, showing how to use skincare products, and doing quick makeovers made me unique. I was not only demonstrating but also teaching them my skills. Thanks to my style of delivering to a big crowd,

BBC Worldwide Radio asked me for an interview. Everyone was happy with the exhibition's success.

I was staying with my girlfriend Madge, whom I normally stayed with when working in the city. But I had made arrangements to stay with Craig on the final day of the exhibition. He came to the exhibition to pick me up. As we were leaving the building, he walked in front of me. So many people said "Well done" to me as I moved through the crowd. Then a well-known promoter stopped me to talk with me. I did not know that Craig had done business with him, and it did not go well when Craig saw me talking to the promoter. Craig walked off and left me. He was nowhere to be seen. I waited for him till I decided he was not coming back, at which time I made my way to my girlfriend's house. The next day I called him, and he told me I should not be talking to the promoter. That was how arrogant he was.

The Afro Hair and Beauty exhibition resulted in the addition of new hair salons in black communities all over England. Fashion designers were having fashion shows every weekend, and beauty competitions increased. Other promoters were inspired. One of them tried to compete with Afro Hair and Beauty, putting on the big Hair and Beauty Exhibition in my hometown. I worked on the exhibition to restore my credibility in my hometown. The community was buzzing. This promoter held a fashion competition, and I encouraged my sister-in-law to take part as she was a great fashion designer. She designed lingerie and came first in her section.

Shades of Black did not last long in the department store. In fact, it went out of business and the Jewish man died. The girl who had talked her way into my job was my sister-in-law's friend, and all of a sudden, she was a fashion designer. She got my sister-in-law to make up her designs to take part in the fashion competition. I need not say any more. The highlight in my hometown did not last very long.

For the second year of the Afro Hair and Beauty exhibition, Dyke & Dryden changed the concept of the show and made it for the general public. They stopped taking care of the professional hair and beauty technicians. It became all about numbers and making money. Everyone was quickly realising that there was a black beauty economy, and everyone was in a race with everyone else to become trained in fashion, hair, and beauty.

Dyke & Dryden had its own retail shop in a shopping centre. I got a contract with them to demonstrate their skincare products and cosmetics in the shopping centre. By this time, my skills came easily to me.

I was staying more regularly with Craig when I was working in the city. He had bought a new house. When he was house-hunting, he had asked me to go along with him to look at the houses, but he never asked me to move in with him again. He was very proud and was not going to forget that I had turned him down before.

Owing to my unique skills, I always had secure work as the black beauty economy grew. The number of professionals increased, and new professionals tried to get their share by pushing out the visionaries. It became more of a rat race. Dyke & Dryden started to change. Their marketing manager, Roger, left and set up his own distribution company. Dyke & Dryden started to make their own products, which were good-quality. Most of the big American companies left them to distribute their products with Roger's new company. He also found an American cosmetic and skincare company called Vera Moore, owned by one of the United States' daytime soap opera actresses. These products were the perfect line to work with. Hollywood Curls had pulled out of the British market and was trading in South Africa and Dubai.

Roger and I started promoting Vera Moore cosmetics up and down the country in salons, on radio shows, and on BBC television. We worked with make-up departments, did a workshop on a new black television station, did fashion shows, and provided training in colleges.

Then Roger decided we would create a new event for professionals, and HairX was born. It was an exciting cutting-edge exhibition for professionals. Vera Moore, along with two of her beautiful make-up assistants, came over. I learned a great deal from them and fitted in well with the team. We had a great exhibition. I was on a high and feeling inspired.

After they left, I had another opportunity to work on a photo shoot for *Black Hair and Beauty Magazine*. I had a very successful shoot with a double-centre page and a front-page spread in colour. And this time when I saw the magazine on the news stand, I was very proud.

I also had another opportunity to showcase in my hometown. I appeared on a lunchtime programme called *Pebble Mill at One*, and during the wedding season, I was booked out.

My relationship with Craig was not going anywhere, and his behaviour was becoming more and more strange. I never knew where I was with him. My relationship with Benny was also not what I wanted. He had fallen in love with me, and I had fallen out of love with him, but I was trying for our son's sake. My parents were selling up and going back to Jamaica.

So many young people were coming into the beauty business, and a lot of back-stabbing was going on. Everyone was trying to get my work and be better than me. I had a girlfriend who had gone to Germany to work in the nightlife industry. She encouraged me to come and try it as it was easy money, adding that German men loved black women. So I decided to go and made some arrangements to have my sister-in-law's sister come and live at my apartment so she could stay with my son at night. He was going to school, so he would be tired. Benny was still working nights, so he could take my son to school and pick him up. At the weekend, if Benny wanted to go out to do his own thing, my son could stay at the house of my brother and his wife.

Chapter 10
My Travels

Now my journey became self-destructive. I decided to, for no reason, go to Germany. I was making a good name for myself in the beauty industry. All I had to do was to stick to it. So why go off on this destructive adventure? As the bottom line was to sell high-class sex, I was going back to my adolescent behaviour. It was destructive and self-abusive. I had no need to do something like this when I was at the height of a good career. I had no reason apart from being driven by the amount of money I could make and the possibility that I might find a rich man. Those were good enough reasons for me to want to do this. I did make sure I'd be back to do the big beauty shows, though.

During my first time in Germany, I went to a city called Koblenz, where one of my friends was dancing. All the nightclubs that offered adult entertainment had accommodations above the clubs for their workers as many of them came from other countries. The owner of the first club I worked at had two nightclubs. The one I worked at was in the city centre. The other was just outside the town centre and was a far busier nightclub than the one where I worked. The club I was working in had lots of entertainment, including strippers (which they called dancers), magicians, and singers. When the live entertainment stopped, there was a big-screen television showing porn movies.

I met a lot of black girls. One happened to be a cousin of my cousins, Pam and Campbell. I was never one for drinking, but now I got men to buy me as much champagne as I could. The champagne bottles came in three sizes: a small bottle called a piccolo, which was just over a glass, a half-bottle, and a full-size bottle. The idea was to get the men to buy champagne and to get rid of it by drinking it or finding a way to throw it away, but still keeping the man interested enough to buy more champagne. You would offer him a little bit of yourself for a larger-size bottle of champagne, which you could drink with him in a private space called 'Separat.' If you managed to get the big bottle, you would get a special room. Sometimes it was in the basement of the club. You were not allowed to have sex on the premises or go with the men privately to their hotels. It was about teasing the man with just enough encouragement to get them to buy you another bottle. And if the man was a big spender and you needed help, you would get another girl to join you. That made it easier as while one occupied the man, the other got rid of the champagne by throwing it into the ice-filled champagne bucket or onto the carpet floor. We were paid a percentage on the bottles of champagne the men bought. When I was working with another girl, we shared the percentage.

Rules were broken. The men knew what they wanted. They all had different needs; that was why they used the club. You had to assess if the man would make a good private client and, if so, arrange to meet him outside of club hours. Sometimes the men would suggest this themselves and make an offer. If you could get one thousand Deutschmarks plus shopping, and if he really had money, you would want him as a boyfriend or a regular date.

At first I was rubbish at it as my heart was not that cold, and you have to be cold to make it in this lifestyle. It was difficult to adapt to the life as I had to try to learn the language, which was a big obstacle. German men were calculating. They knew what they had come for, and they were cold-hearted.

While in Koblenz, I dated two young men. They both spoke good English and were soldiers. One was from a rich background. The other could not afford to buy champagne and had strong political views.

I also became friendly with an interesting man who looked like a tidy tramp. He was very clean, wore Jesus sandals with socks, drove a diesel Mercedes, had pale skin, and wore corduroy trousers and a leather jacket that he called his second skin. He had no children and was separated from his wife, who was living in the Black Forest with a group of people. He was a workaholic computer engineer employed at a big engineering brand. He worked every day, even on Christmas Day. He never checked his bank account to see how much money he had; he did not know how much the company paid him. He lived in a beautiful apartment and suffered from guilt that through his knowledge and inventions, he was changing the world, but not for the best. He was good company. Either I would stay over in his beautiful apartment or he would travel to see me at the weekend wherever I was working in Germany, and he took me to expensive restaurants.

I made sure that I worked as close as I could to

the Swiss border so that I visit Sharon as often as I could. Or if I were to run into any trouble, I could easily get to safety and stay with her until I could find an appropriate club to work at. One of the clubs I worked at was not only on the Swiss border but also on the French border. It was very busy with lots of Chinese men and gangs of beautiful young men from Poland and the former Yugoslavia. These young men were quite dangerous. They looked like a million dollars scrubbed up, as if they had just stepped off the page of a magazine to attract the new girls. And before you knew it, they would have you working as a sex slave. The first I learned about their method, I was talking to one of them, when one of the girls who permanently worked at the club came over to me. She got me away from him and told me about such activities. This was something I had to become aware of if I was going to work in this kind of environment.

The second hard experience I had was at a club that was run by a husband and wife. After my second day working there, the husband used his kcys to enter my room while I was sleeping. He got into my bed and forced me to have sex. The next day, his wife threw me out. I had to call Sharon. I sat waiting on a bench by the road in a small village for her husband to come get me.

I developed a routine of working three months and then returning to England for one month. Each time I returned to Germany, I tried a new nightclub. My girlfriends who were dancers would get me to come and work at the clubs they were dancing in. As dancers, they only stayed at a club for one month and then moved on. A lot of rich Arab men used the nightclubs. Sometimes a super-rich Arab would come and close down the club, giving the owner some serious money for us all to drink champagne. Some had funny requests, such as asking the girls who were on their periods to take off their bloody sanitary pads, place them on a gold plate, and put a crisp white napkin around his neck. The girl whose sanitary pad was being eaten had to watch it being eaten with a gold knife and fork. One Arab man requested poo, also eating it from a gold plate with a gold knife and fork. The girl who was able to poo on the plate also had to watch. Luckily for me, I never got in that position, but the girls who were able to accommodate those kinds of requests were given large tips.

I did get a really nice German man who bought me champagne and asked me not to throw it away. He got me a full bottle so he could go to the separat room. He asked me not to go to the toilet as he wanted me to pee in his mouth, saying that this was how he liked to drink champagne. That act came with a big private tip for me.

I met a handsome, rich Australian sheep farmer. We became good friends over the years, and he asked me to marry him. He was a member of the same Rotary Club as my African prince. Of course, neither of them knew this.

I met another handsome German man who was an aviation engineer. We started spending lots of time together with his friend and his friend's wife. They had a boat and lived in Switzerland. On Sundays, we joined his friends in Switzerland to do fun things.

My parents were now settled in Jamaica, and we planned our first family trip back to Jamaica with my son, my second-eldest brother, my younger sister, and their families. This would be the first time returning to Jamaica since all those years ago when I left as a dying child to have my life-saving operation. I would be returning not only alive, but also with a healthy son. Seeing Jamaica—my beautiful country—with a fresh pair of eyes, I was overwhelmed by its beauty and its growing economy. I started planning in my head; with the next big money I earned from Germany, I would return to Jamaica to set up a skincare business in one of the hotels on the north coast.

When I returned to England, I had made up my mind that I was going to leave Benny. I could not allow my son to see his abusive behaviour anymore. He was calling me at night, threatening to come and hurt me. I pushed my furniture against the front door at night, my five-year-old son with his little legs helping me to push. He would say, "Push, Mummy. We don't want Daddy to come and hurt you when we are sleeping." He would wake up early to help me put the furniture back. When Benny came home, my son would talk to him nicely, so he did not come and bother me. I asked my second-eldest brother if I could move in with him and his family. Finally, on a weekend when Benny was away, I moved out, taking only clothes to my brother's house. I left Benny the apartment I had been making plans to buy for seven thousand pounds. The value of the apartment now would be enormous, but I did not want Benny to say I had made him homeless. He was devastated.

My son comforted me that first night in our new home. He said, "Mummy, this is better. Now I can love you both separately."

After settling my son into his new school while living with my brother and his family, I went off to

Germany to make some more money. I didn't know how many more trips I could make to Germany as I was getting a little tired of the lifestyle. I was still seeing the young German aviation engineer. He was fun.

Whenever I returned to England, I made sure I did a few events in the city. I also missed Craig, and I could feel his strong energy and that he was ready for me. I was praying that he missed me too. I was ready to settle down with him if he would ask me again.

I had an event in the city on a Saturday. The plan was to stay with Craig after the event. I was hoping that he would ask me not only to move in but also to marry him. I felt strongly that he was ready to ask me. As I was leaving the house to catch my train, the postman arrived, and there was a letter for me from my young German aviation engineer with some photos of us on the Alps, our bodies very close together. The fashion for handbags at the time was small bags, and I still tried to fit as much as I could in the small bag I was carrying. I took the letter from the postman and shoved it and the photos into my bag so I could read the letter and look at the photos on the train.

After the event, Craig and I settled down to a perfect night of making love. After making love, he was just in the flow to pop the question to me, when I jumped off the bed to go to the toilet. There beside the bed, I had left my handbag open with the letter and photos in clear view. When I returned to the room, his mood had changed to one of coldness. I knew he had taken the letter from my bag and looked at the photos. The moment was lost.

I had planned another trip, this time to Baden-

Baden, the rich playground of Germany. I was taking a flight from the city, and Craig wanted to come to the airport to see me off. This was not his normal behaviour towards me. We planned to have breakfast, but I had a feeling it was not for any good reason. Sure enough, he wanted me to know he had seen the photos and was not happy I was seeing a white man. He felt I was disrespecting him. I could understand his feelings; I felt bad because I knew that waiting at the other end of the flight was my German boyfriend whom he had seen in the photos. I didn't know how I was going to save even our friendship. We ordered breakfast, and he asked questions. I can't remember what excuse I gave him.

I enjoyed my time working in Baden-Baden. It was very rich in culture, money, and famous people. It had the best spas, the best casinos, the best restaurants, the best retail shops, and the best nightclub I ever worked in. It was owned by an Israeli man with a heart. The manager of the club was a tall, sexy Polish man married to a beautiful German woman who was the house dancer and his extra eyes and ears. The manager also had the most handsome nephew, who had started working there at the same time as me. He was the bartender, and we got close, sleeping together most nights. He helped me to get rid of the champagne if I was drinking at the bar, or when he knew the champagne the waitress had ordered was for me, he made sure he got rid of one glass in the ice bucket. He was also my party buddy. After work we would go to a discotheque in France and dance till morning.

I mostly ate at the same restaurant in the evening, not too far from the club where I was staying. I also ate with some friends and a gentleman who was a film score composer. He also visited the club and bought me champagne, and I sometimes visited him at his house, where he lived with his girlfriend and worked in his recording studio.

His girlfriend was a photographer. She got me to model for her and took some beautiful black-and-white pictures of me. She exhibited them in a gallery in Germany.

There was one Israeli man who came to the club almost every night. He had beautiful grey hair and olive skin. He would buy you a drink if he felt like it. I fell for his beauty the first time I saw him. He always wore white and called me *darling*. He always wanted to feel my skin and said it was like silk. He tried to get me to meet him during the day at the sauna, but I never went even though I liked him very much. And I am glad I followed that little voice not to go. My Polish boyfriend informed me that he owned three brothels in Baden-Baden and was a human trafficker, selling women to rich men as sex slaves. He was gently trying to groom me. I told tell him one day that I knew what he did. He had this tiny, beautiful, very cold German girlfriend who ran the brothels, and she always gave me a dirty look whenever she saw me. He and I ended up being good friends, and he often invited me to the South of France, where he had his hotels and yacht. I was always joking with him that I did not want to be sold.

I made so many friends in Baden-Baden and had the best time ever in Germany.

On my return to England from Baden-Baden, I decided not to return to Germany again. I was preoccupied with the wedding season in my hometown and with fashion shows in the city. Roger kept me busy, but I had time to have a good social life and make new friends in the city, as well as spend time with my son, taking him to and from school. One of the new friends I made was Julie, a talented up-and-coming fashion designer who would later play a big role in my life.

I was seeing an older black gentleman in my hometown. He got me an evening job working in the community social club, of which he was part owner. We went out for late-night dinners and on occasion he booked a country hotel for us to spend time together in. He thought he had me exclusively. He did not realise I was far too professional for him, and he did not have the kind of money I was used to getting from men. He was a little tight with his money.

One night he was unable to pick me up from the club, so I took the opportunity to go off with a younger man who was new to the community. He took me home, and we became lovers. Of course, I lost the job, but it was just a job to help my social life as the nightlife was still in my system.

I met a white man through a girlfriend. He was an ex-policeman, and he loved black women. We started dating, but I was not the only black woman he was seeing. He knew what he was looking for and chose a black girl to front his business. I did not know that he was the man behind one of the most established beauty salons and beauty schools in my hometown. I had worked with his partner many times. I also found out that it was not just a business relationship; she was his live-in partner. Once I found out what he was about, I dropped him.

My friend Leon opened a beautiful wine bar

restaurant in the community l had grown up in. Sharon was visiting from Switzerland at the time, so she and I attended the grand opening. The best of the community from far and wide attended the opening. Among all these beautiful people was a beautiful black man who looked very much like Craig. Sharon called him over to have a drink with us, and we found out he was a footballer and played for a league team. At the end of the night, he drove me home in a beautiful red sports car. He was very keen to see me, so the next day we went on our first date to a beautiful wine bar. We sat in its exquisite garden and talked. He was the kind of man I could fall in love with, and he came with all the right credentials. We saw each other every day for a week, and we finally ended up at his beautiful house one evening, where things got heated. He was more than six feet tall and had muscles in all the right places. Passion was running hot. He picked me up very easily, carried me upstairs, and laid me on his bed. He was in control, our passion now at boiling point. I could not find or feel his penis, but I gave the best performance of my life. It made him feel good, but that was the end of him for me. I was not interested in seeing him again after that night. He called me every day, but I was lucky and was never the one to answer the phone. When he called, he was told I was not at home. Then one evening I was upstairs, looking out the bedroom window, and saw his red sports car coming up my street. I told my nephew, who answered the door, to tell him I was not in. He did not call me again. I suppose he was used to being let down.

I had stayed friends with my girlfriend Karen, who had worked in the store with me. Just after I gave birth to my son, she went off to the United States to live with her father, who she had not seen for years. We had always kept in touch over the years by letter and one day I received a letter from her informing me she was moving to Florida and getting married. I wrote back to her to say I was going to Jamaica to set up a skincare business and she replied saying that I should consider coming to Florida and living with her. She also had a son, and she informed me that Florida was just like Jamaica. Besides, according to Karen, a flight to Jamaica from Florida was only one hour and fifteen minutes. She felt I would do better setting up my business in Florida as it was just being developed and because my skills would go down well there. My son was six years old around this time. I had gotten him a telescope, and he spent nights looking at the stars. He decided he wanted to be an astronaut and that we should go to live in Florida as that's where NASA was. So when Karen asked me to come to Florida, it felt like the perfect opportunity. I talked it over with my son. He wanted to make the sacrifice for me to go to Florida and prepare a new life for him.

Out of the blue, Craig decided he wanted to meet my family. One Sunday he drove to my hometown to meet my son and my brother and his family. During the visit it came up in conversation that I wanted to go to the United States. I was hoping Craig would say no, that I should come and live with him, but he didn't. Instead, he said, "You will need a visa." He told me to give him my passport, adding that he would get a visa for me. I took the chance and gave him my passport. He left that Sunday evening, and by Thursday, my passport came back in the post with a multiple visa for the United States.

After receiving my passport with a visiting and working visa for the United States, Craig was not going to let go of the challenge. Whenever I talked to him, he asked me, "When are you going to America?" My son and I talked it over and over again; I wanted to make sure he understood what was ahead of us. All he wanted was for us to go to the United States so he could have his dream to become an astronaut or an aviator.

Karen was now settled in Florida and married. She was keen for me to join her. I had made up my mind to go, but I still had to make all the plans as I would be away for six months. During this period, I was seeing more of Leon, dating him a few nights a week. It was fun as it was a champagne lifestyle at the best places in town. He drove the best vintage cars. By this time, he had closed his wine bar restaurant.

I made arrangements to go to the United States but still had some work commitments that I had to finish. But it was all coming together for me to leave. The week before I was due to leave for Florida, I went out with Leon. He picked me up in a beautiful vintage car, and we went to one of the best nightclubs in town, where the who's who hung out. It was champagne all night. We took up positions at the bar, me sitting on a bar stool and Leon standing beside me. I was mixing my champagne with orange juice and enjoying all the attention I was getting from Leon and his friends. The club was getting full and was in full swing.

Then, in the crowd, I spotted a man looking at me intensely. This man was making sure I saw him. He would not stop staring at me. When I managed to get a good look at him, I saw it was Mr Footballer. He knew I had seen him. He knew that sooner or later, I would need to go to the toilet. I looked over to the bathrooms and saw that Mr Footballer was stood the entrance to the ladies' toilet. I tried to hold out, hoping he would give up. At long last, he moved away. I made my way to the toilet and used it. But on my way out, Mr Footballer was waiting for me. Of course, he wanted to know why he was not able to get hold of me. My excuses were viable—I had been working away and getting ready to leave for the United States in the next week, and I was having a going-away drink with Leon. But I promised him I would keep in touch with him from the United States. I never saw or heard from him again.

At the end of the night, I had drunk so much champagne that I wanted to be sick. I was staying the night at Leon's house. We barely made it to his house without me being sick in his vintage car. I ended up being sick all over his beautiful bathroom floor. I don't know how I made it through the next day as I had to get home and pack so I could get on the train to work on a fashion show in the city.

So the day came for me to go on my new adventure to Florida with seven hundred pounds in my pocket. I got the early coach from my town to the city airport and got my flight to Florida. Karen met me at the airport, and my American life began. Florida was just in the early stages of being developed into the state it is now. Then it was swampy, dusty, sandy, and dry. During the eighties, Florida was a cocaine hotspot where killings carried long prison sentences.

My passport was stamped for six months. Karen had a nice three-bedroom apartment, and Florida's tropical weather was like Jamaica without the mountains. I was not impressed with the people, and there was clearly segregation. This was not the life I was used to. I was likely not going to find a job in skincare. It was my intention to use my skills and qualifications as a beauty therapist, but black people didn't know anything about looking after their skin. And to work in the skincare profession in the United States, I would have to apply for a state licence. At that time, my only option was to go back to beauty school, and they were charging big money for the course. The only thing I would be allowed to do without a licence was applying make-up, doing eyebrow arching, and selling make-up and skincare products. I had no idea how my challenges were going to work out.

There was no pavement to walk on. The bus stop had no seat or shelter from the rain or hot sun, and the bus only came every hour. There were plenty of lizards and mosquitoes. When it rained, all the sand would climb up the walls of the houses. Everything was bigger than me. There were no yellow cabs in Florida, unlike in New York, where you could flag down a cab on the street. In Florida, cabs would only pick you up from an address.

I was very keen to enjoy the nightlife in Florida, so Karen took me to a black nightclub. It was OK, but I wanted the real American experience. She was not doing much partying, so she asked one of her friends who partied to take me out. She had gone to beauty school with this friend, but she did not know her very well. We went to a mixed nightclub downtown with people from different cultures. At some point during the night, her boyfriend turned up and hit on me. He was not driving, so when she took me home, he was with us and therefore found out where I lived. By the end of the night, I knew he was a pilot with a light aeroplane licence. He was from a small Caribbean island in the West Indies, not far from Florida. His father was prime minister of this island. He was young, showing off, and spending big money.

My first encounter with danger in Florida was also with him. As I was not working, I stayed at home by myself during the day. It had been around four weeks since I arrived in Florida, when one day I heard really hard banging on the front door. It became very urgent, as if it were the police. When I looked through the spyhole in the door, I recognised him. When he asked me if he could come in, I don't know what possessed me, but I opened the door. He was standing there, sweat pouring off him, his shirt open and exposing his chest, and a gun stuck in his pants. He pushed past me and came into the house. I could not believe what was happening. I asked him what was going on, why he was there, and he said he had to crash his light aeroplane as he was being chased by police helicopters for flying a drug run. He had been running and hiding, and he needed to come here and catch his breath. All I could think of was the apartment being surrounded by police with guns, dogs, and helicopters, the cops yelling, "You are surrounded. Come out with your hands up."

I told him he had to go as it was not my house. He asked me to give him a few minutes more, and then, thank God, he left. My heart was pounding as I knew some American police officers were not nice; they shot first and asked questions later. I never saw that man again.

Some months later, while working in a salon, one of

the girls I worked with was from the same island as him. The island was having a beauty contest, and all the contestants had come to Florida to get their hair and make-up done, so I got the chance to ask about him. I was told he was doing well and not flying any more.

Karen had a friend who was a lecturer at a university whose side job was selling health insurance to companies. He asked me to work for him, using my English accent to call companies and arrange appointments for him to go and see them. He paid me cash weekly so I could pay my rent.

I had to find a salon I could work in applying make-up, doing eyebrow arching, and selling skincare products. I found a beauty salon downtown, which was the top black beauty salon in the city. Owned by a family of sisters, the salon was called Ahead of Times. They loved me. I started to work Thursday and Friday evenings, and all day Saturdays. While working there, I met two girls who became my friends. Alice, a hairdresser, was from South America, and Lora was from Jamaica. It was a very busy salon as everybody who was anybody patronised it. I was busy as a make-up artist, creating new looks for the clients. All black women in Florida wore red lipstick. There was no variation in colour, so I had to move them away from using red lipstick and get them to shape their eyebrows. As soon as they finished having their hair done, they would use my service, sometimes twice a week. They kept me busy. I was using Vera Moore cosmetics as they were easy to get from New York. I also sold the skincare and make-up line, which is how I was making my money. Doing my two jobs kept me busy.

To get to the salon, I had to take two long bus rides. Sometimes Karen came and picked me up if she was free in the evenings and I had to work late at the salon.

Before I left England, I had met a Jamaican banker. He was working in England, getting Jamaicans to open bank accounts in Jamaica to save money. We liked each other but had not had enough time to go out, so we arranged to meet in Florida while he was there doing business. We arranged to spend Christmas Day together.

For my first Thanksgiving in the United States, Karen's husband's half-sister invited us all to have dinner with her family. This was the first time I had heard about Thanksgiving.

It was like a Christmas celebration at Thanksgiving dinner. The sister's uncle Robert was there. He was eight years older than me, and he took a liking to me straightaway. He had not long before this moved to Florida from Chicago. He was not a bad-looking man, he was tall, and I found him sexually attractive. He was not the type of man I could fall in love with, but I could have great sex with him. AIDS had just become the biggest death sentence for everyone, and I needed to find one sexual partner while I was in Florida. Robert was a Jamaican, so he was perfect for my sexual needs. He could not wait to spend time with me. We made a date for the next day.

He took me to a bar that had big boats docked on the pier. He was living in a hotel downtown, not far from the beach. It was one of those hotels that used to be a five star in its heyday, but the management had let the hotel run down. People were using it to do all kind of things. All night you could hear people shouting and fighting. Robert kept his room untidy and dark, but the light from the street shone into the room.

But it was some of the best sex I had, with no inhibitions. I felt like one of those prostitutes who were not far from the room. My sexual imagination was off the scale. Robert didn't stop once all night. I made sure I told him he was not the kind of man I wanted to fall in love with or have a deep relationship with, I just wanted him to be my sexual partner. I also told Robert I had a boyfriend who was going to visit me on Christmas Day.

He agreed, but in the next few days, I could see he was not right in the head. He started to stalk me. He worked as a car salesman during the day and a bartender at night. I later found out that he had worked as a bartender in Chicago too.

The distance between where I was living and where I was working was long. After my first date with Robert, I was walking to the bus stop to go to work, and who was driving slowly behind me? Robert. He wanted to drive me to work. I said no, adding that I was happy to take the bus. But he was not taking no for an answer. He followed the bus and kept pulling alongside it, begging me to get off the bus. Finally, the other passengers started to get involved, saying to me, "Come on, loves. Go with him." I never got off the bus. He followed me all the way to work. So now he knew where I was working. Then he turned up after I finished work. I never went with him. One morning I found him sleeping in his car under my bedroom window. After that, I never went on another date with him.

Nevertheless, Robert was stalking me and

followed my bus downtown to where I worked at the salon. I had totally forgotten I had told Robert that a boyfriend was joining me for Christmas. Early on Christmas morning, Robert turned up at the apartment and would not leave. Karen and her husband told him I was not in, but he did not believe them and would not go. I sat in the wardrobe almost all day. He did finally leave, and I was able to go and meet my Jamaican banker. My relationship with the banker never got off to a start.

Then a wonderful opportunity came my way— the Miss Florida competition. Ahead of Times was doing the contestants' and celebrities' hair. Racism was still rampant in the United States during this period, and Florida was no exception. This part of the competition was for black contestants, who were all college women. There were no black make-up artists and seeing as I was doing the make-up in the salon, I got the job to do the make-up for the contestants, after they did their hair. I wrote down the colours I used on them so I could touch up their make-up before the show. I only expected to do the contestants' make-up before the show, but then they asked me to do the celebrities' make-up too. The list of celebrities included Stevie Wonder, Denzel Washington, Miss America, Bunny De Barge, and the radio celebrity Jane Carnegie. I didn't have the time to enjoy meeting these celebrities and had no pictures of me doing their make-up. I was doing so much by myself. My experience working at the big beauty exhibitions in England helped me to do this beauty competition single-handedly.

Stevie Wonder was very difficult to make up. He had one of those big keyboards in his lap and was playing and moving his head from side to side and up and down. He would not keep still till I spoke to him like a mother would speak to her child who was acting up. He was so shocked that he put the keyboard away and kept still. He asked me where I was from. When I told him England, he said if ever he was in England and I was there, I should look him up as he would never forget me because no one normally challenged him.

Denzel Washington was a darling. His wife was with him. They had just come back from a skiing holiday, and he had a tan everywhere except around his eyes, which had been protected by his goggles. He looked like a raccoon.

The office I was working from for the lecturer was on the side of the church he attended. Coincidentally, it was the same branch of the church my parents attended in England and which I had spent some of my youth attending. The pastor of his church was also the pastor who had taken over the church I attended in England after I stopped going to it. I kept well out of sight, making sure that I did not bump into the pastor or the members as I knew some of them. Of course, the lecturer and I got around to having a sexual relationship. But as he was one of those men who pre-ejaculates, he just made a mess all over me. I told him that if he wanted any more sex from me, he had to give me oral sex. I knew he wouldn't do it, so he stopped asking me for sex.

With Florida's hot sun, I started wanting sex and gave into Robert's persistence. The lecturer I was working for moved me into this nice glass office building on the tenth floor. There were other high-rise glass office buildings to the left and right of the building I was working in. Robert would come to the office, get under the desk while I was on the phone, and give me oral sex. I was addicted to his sex. It became more daring as he put me on top of the desk and had sex with me. I felt as if I was in the clouds. Turning around, I could see the other office buildings. I did not know whether anyone could see us from their offices; that made it more exciting.

I found a beauty school through an ad in the local paper. The owner was a tall, beautiful, white American lady, and we got on. She was only teaching nails and make-up but was in the process of teaching skincare. We agreed that I would teach her make-up class, and she said I could sit in on her class for the Florida state law. She told me I should buy a beauty therapist's workbook and teach myself the American beauty method. She would sign off on the hours of training, along with the state law, and then I could apply for the examination. It did not take me long to study the American beauty therapist methods and apply for the examination.

The time on my visa to stay in the United States was running out; I had already completed six months. My intention was to go back to England, stay two weeks, and return to the United States. I don't know why I gave Robert my phone number in England, but I did.

I returned to England and decided to take my son to Switzerland. I had not gotten in touch with Craig for the six months I was away. When I returned, he was not too impressed with me as I had never called him when I was away. When I told him I was going to Switzerland, he thought I was going to see my white boyfriend there. He asked me to stop by his shop to see him on my way to the airport, but I could not as

I was travelling with my son. I was also on a budget, and I was not going to ask him to cover the extra journey costs. So he promised me that he would come and see me when I got back from Switzerland. I did call him while I was in Switzerland, but he was funny with me.

Then one day I had a call from Robert while I was in Switzerland. He had called the number in England I had given him, and whomever he'd spoken to had given him my number in Switzerland. He started calling me there every day. He said he had gotten a divorce and that as soon as I got back to Florida, he would marry me so I could get my permanent resident's green card. That would make it easier for me to stay in the United States. At the time, I was more interested in Craig and looking forward to seeing him as soon as I got back to England.

When I returned to England, I called Craig, and he assured me that he was going to come and see me at the weekend. I waited all weekend, till eleven o'clock Sunday night, then I called him. He answered and asked me why I was calling his house so late, adding that I was not to call him again. I put the phone down in shock. I had heard him talking to women that way before, and I had promised myself if ever he treated me that way, it would be over. On Monday morning, I bought my ticket to go back to Florida. I froze all my feelings for Craig and focused on getting back to Florida, taking up Robert's offer to marry him, getting my green card and building a successful business. I wanted to show Craig that I did not need him and that I was going to make it work.

When I arrived in Florida, it was strange and frightening to have Robert meeting me at the airport instead of Karen. He had gotten an apartment across from Karen's apartment. If I had not arranged things the way I had, I would have changed my mind as it was pure madness. That was not how I wanted to experience being married.

I arrived in Florida on Tuesday, and by Thursday morning, I was downtown at the courthouse, getting married, with strangers as witnesses. After we did it, we went to some posh place to eat. I was unemotional. I told Robert I would be a good wife to him, but I would not be able to fall in love with him the way he wanted me to love him. Of course, he pretended he was OK with it, saying that he just wanted to help me. I found out later that he had used my desire to get a green card to get me to be his wife.

The first encounter with this madness of Robert's did not take long. A few days after I'd started living with him, we were talking in bed one night, getting to know each other. We were talking about our past experiences. I can't remember why, but he got jealous of my life, and we got into an argument. Things got sour. I got out of bed and went into the living room. I lay on the sofa to cool off and fell asleep. I really thought I was dreaming. I felt a sharp pain in my side. I woke up as I felt another pain in my side. And there he was, standing over me, kicking me in my side. I grabbed his penis as he was about to kick me again. He begged me to let go and said he just wanted me to come back to bed. I told him no way, not after he had done this to me.

That was the start of four years of madness and abuse. This was the man who used to pick me up from work and sleep outside my bedroom window. Now he would not take me anywhere or pick me up from work. He would watch me walk in the hot sun to catch a bus. The only thing we had in common was sex.

When I applied for my beauty therapist exam, the owner of the nail school suggested I send a copy of my English qualification along with my application to the Beauty Therapist Association. It seemed my qualifications had become international; the United States was using the same association qualifications. So I did not have to sit the exam. My beauty licence was sent to me, and I was able to start my skincare business.

I bought some used equipment from a hotel, and Ahead of Times gave me a space to work. But they did not understand what doing a facial was about and the privacy I needed to give the clients. As they did not have the appropriate space, I had to look for a salon with the right space. I found a salon closer to where I lived that had a nice room. The clients I had would be comfortable there. Charm's Salon was owned by a Jamaican lady. She had two children and a niece whom she had working at the salon and in her house. She was the kind of woman who liked to be in the now, but she treated her niece like Cinderella.

I settled in and was building a nice clientele. Black people were beginning to understand the value of having facials. I got radio and television exposure, and my European facial techniques were spreading fast in the black community as the new trend.

Karen worked at a heart hospital. She met a little old lady who was a patient there. This old lady was cute and full of life. She encouraged Karen to visit her home and meet some of her girlfriends. She said they got together, read the Bible, shared knowledge, and ate food. Karen asked me to go with her to visit the old lady and her friends. The lady encouraged us to join a group, the Florida women's chapter of the Freemasons. I had heard about this organisation just before I left England. It sounded interesting, but when I was faced with the possibility of joining them, I had become a little more mature. Having learned some facts about them, I was not keen on being part of a secret society. In the group of women we met, there was one lady who looked very suspicious. She kept talking to us with her eyes. My heart was guiding me and said not to do this, it was not for me.

The old lady worked on manipulating us to join their sisterhood chapter. She told us we had plenty of time to think about it as they only did their initiation twice a year, when the grand master of their chapter came to Florida. Then she told us that he was coming to Florida sooner than they expected and would be holding an initiation in two weeks. For initiation, we were told we had to wear black and white—black shoes, white gloves, black skirts and white blouses—and that Karen would not be in a fit state to drive after the initiation. The week before the initiation, they had a big dance, which Karen and I attended. During the evening, a woman came up to us. She knew we were planning to get initiated, and in a very angry voice, she told us not to get involved with these people as they were the devil.

On the Monday morning of the week we were due to be initiated, I went to the mall to buy black and white clothes, as these were not the colours I normally wore. I could not find any black and white clothes, not even a pair of black shoes. I got fed up and gave up looking. When I got to work, I learned that one of my male clients, a minister, had called and left a message for me to call him so he could come in for a facial. Before he arrived, I called Karen and told her I had changed my mind and would not be getting initiated into this secret society. We agreed that we would go and see the old lady that evening and tell her we were not interested in joining their group.

During the minister's facial, I asked him what he knew about the Freemasons as a friend of mine was planning to join. He almost jumped off the bed as he said, "For the love of God, tell your friend not to sell her soul!" That was good enough for me. I had a feeling he knew that friend was me, as he prayed for me before he left.

That night we went to see the old lady to tell her we would not be joining. The lady who had kept talking to us with her eyes, for the first time, felt her spirit was lifted, and she was at peace.

My business was going well. The only problem was the environment. The owner of Charm's Salon was very abusive to her niece in front of the clients. She just had a big ego. One day she tore strips off her niece in front of a full salon. One of my clients was there and was in shock and concerned about the young lady, who left in a flood of tears. No one could intervene as it would have been at a cost for anyone to challenge the owner's behaviour.

The next day the owner was away from the salon for most of the day. I was sitting at the reception desk when the phone rang. My client who had witnessed the owner's aggressive behaviour was calling me with concern to see how the niece was doing. Little did I know that a client of the owner, one I had never seen before, was waiting for her in the reception area and listening to my conversation, which was in no way unfair. The client told the owner that I was talking about her. The owner wasted no time in asking me to leave.

Not far from where I was living, a young man was opening a high-class beauty salon called Tender Heart Salon. I met with Leroy, the owner of Tender Heart Salon, and secured to rent the facial room when they opened. There would be two parts to the salon. On one side was the spa with the sauna, massage, nails, and facials. That would be the side I would be working on. The other side was for hairdressing and barbering. That side was owned by Leroy. My side was owned by Cornell. He was a known drug dealer and had just gotten out of prison. He was using the salon to launder his money. Cornell and Leroy were working together, but the businesses were separate. All the hairstylists and nail technicians who worked at Tender Heart Salon were the best in Florida, and everyone worked for themselves. Their clientele were professional drug dealers and their partners had lots of disposable income.

During the eighties, Florida was all about drugs, and you never knew who was who. There were lots of killings every day. I knew some of the people who had been killed, and it was never in a nice way. I was greatly upset to hear a client's partner, the father of her three children, had been jailed for drugs and given a seventeen-year prison sentence. He had left her with millions of his money. She had regular facials with me and used to come in with about six young bodyguards. She started messing around with a Jamaican radio presenter. Her partner was not happy about this, so he had the presenter executed. They put matchsticks under his nails and lit them. They cut out both his eyes. They cut off his penis and stuck it in his mouth. They left him to die in his Jeep.

Her jailed partner was still not happy with her. He hired gunmen to kill her. At a traffic light, with their children in the back of the car, the gunman pulled up to her car and shot her in the head. When I heard the news, I was traumatised.

Then there was a gun battle outside Tender Heart Salon involving Cornell, and he was killed. Luckily for me, I was not at the salon that day. That side of the salon was closed, and Leroy moved me to his side. He turned the room in which they were doing weaves into a facial room for me.

I had a young male client from England who was on the run from New York. He came every day for a facial and would give me a big tip. He used the time to sleep and always had his hands on his gun. He finally moved on.

All these drug dealers had so much disposable money that they had to spend it. I did get close to one of my drug-dealing clients. His girlfriend worked for the postal service and came for facials too. They had a couple of children. He would come every other day for his facial. He decided to invest in an R&B music group and I worked for him, doing the make-up for their album cover.

The drug dealers were always going "out of town," which is what they called it when they were going to do a drug deal. The one I had gotten close to went "out of town" and was killed. Some drug dealers, if they got friendly with you, might ask you to keep their money at your house and pay you for doing it.

There were lots of undercover police, some of whom

would pose as your clients and pretend they were drug dealers. They asked you to keep their money. If you said yes, they arrested you, and then you would get a long stay in jail. This happened to Alice, my hairdresser's girlfriend's sister. She got a fifteen-year prison sentence. During this time, I was never approached by anyone to do anything.

Lora and Alice both worked with me at Tender Heart Salon. I was good friends with both of them as we had all worked at Ahead of Times Salon previously, and Alice and I had both worked at Charm's Salon too.

Leroy, the owner of Tender Heart Salon, was a tall, big, handsome young man. He was gentle and had a great personality in every way. He also worked as a bodyguard in the music industry and was away a lot. His mother was a typical American black woman from Georgia. She ran the salon when he was not there. Along with two other male family members, they kept the salon clean. As soon as hair dropped on the floor, it was swept up. Their duties were to run the reception area, keep the salon clean, and do the laundry. They also had the secret job of protecting the salon.

One of my clients was the Channel 5 News anchor woman. Her best friend, Maureen, presented a weekly television talk show, and I was invited to be a guest on the show. I ended up doing Maureen's make-up for the show every week. I became good friends with Maureen and her husband. Her husband worked for me, writing my business plan, as my intention was to open a beauty centre using a one-stop business model. I was making a name for myself as a skincare specialist and make-up artist. Having a British background was more than helpful as it enabled me to build trust as a skincare specialist. Everyone was going to the dermatologist for their skin problems, and Mary Kay Cosmetics used consultants to show people to cleanse, tone, and moisturise, calling this a facial.

My friendship with one of my young clients developed. She had the right qualities to be a top model. I worked with her as her make-up artist. We had fun doing early-morning photo shoots. Sometimes we had to start at four in the morning to be ready to catch the first light of day on the beach or some other outdoor backdrop. Sometimes there were late-evening shoots catching the light at twilight. We did shoots in studios or outdoor locations. We had so much fun. She was beautiful, funny, and the happiest, most caring person I have ever known. We have remained friends to this day.

The world is not as big as we think it is. Our lives are all purposeful, and I believe that life is not a series of coincidences. One of my clients from South Africa introduced me to one of her work colleagues, Tom. It so happened he was someone I had known in England. He had relocated to Florida with his wife and two boys. I got reacquainted, not just with him, but also with his wife and boys. I knew him better than I knew his wife, though I knew her from working in the department store. She was a customer I had served, and I waited at the bus stop with her. Karen, Tom, his family, and my South African client started spending fun times together.

I was meeting a lot of English people at the salon, and Tom also met some through his work as an insurance broker. Among the challenges I faced trying to settle down in Florida was that because I was not from the same country, it was hard to get people to share information with me, mostly involving immigration issues for those of us who had married Americans to get green cards. I suggested to Tom and Karen that, as we were already meeting for pool parties and barbecues, we form an association as a vehicle for us to share information and help each other survive in the United States. So we formed the British Expatriate Society of Togetherness (BEST). We continued to meet, adding more members.

One of the biggest events we planned was for the Fourth of July, Independence Day. We had more than one hundred and fifty people. We sold tickets to the British, West Indians, and Americans. We held the event in a big park with other groups and family events. We had such a great day, playing reggae music, eating good food, and playing volleyball. We had a British team against an American team. The whole park got involved. Even Robert turned up.

I became good friends with a girl from England. We played tennis about four times a week. We were around the same age and had plenty of things in common.

I filled in my immigration papers myself, but things did not go as quickly as I would have liked, and Robert was getting crazier. He was still working as both a car salesman and a bartender. And he also carried a gun.

I had gone to a BEST meeting with Karen, and on our return, she had stopped off at her house before dropping me home. When we drove up to her house, we saw her husband picking up clothes from all over their lawn. As we got out of the car and got closer,

I recognised my clothes. Her husband told us that Robert had come by and thrown my clothes all over the lawn. I called the police and made a report. That was the first time I had called the police and reported him. The law was that if I reported him for abuse three times, I would automatically get my green card as it was classified as domestic violence.

I stayed with Karen for a week. Of course, Robert begged me to come home. Eventually, I did go back to the apartment. I also started going to a church with one of my clients. One Sunday when I got back from church, as soon as I closed the front door, Robert ripped off my clothes and accused me of being at church and having sex with the pastor. Rather than taking me to work in his car, again he watched me walk in the hot sun while he followed me in his car, just to see if I talked to anyone or stopped somewhere before I got to work.

One day Roger called me from England. As I was not at home, Robert answered the call. He took Roger's number so I could call him back, but after Robert had spoken with him, he called him back and abused Roger, telling him not to call me again. He paced from the house to his car with his gun. Because of the gun, I was afraid of being asleep when he got home late in the morning. As soon as I heard him coming, I woke up, got out of bed, and went into the walk-in wardrobe as I had visions of him walking in and shooting me while I was asleep.

He always wanted sex when he got home. One of those times I was not in the mood, and we struggled. He bit me deeply on my arms, causing it to bleed. He told me to leave his house, so I called Karen to come and get me. She said she was going to call the police, and she did. A policewoman called me back and said I should stay on the line; the police would be there shortly. Robert, having guessed what was happening, quickly put on his clothes, grabbed his gun, and ran out of the apartment. He got as far as his car before he was surrounded by police with lots of guns. I heard a knock at the door. When I opened the door, a police officer told me they had arrested Robert and needed me to identify him by giving them a description of him, which I did. The policeman looked at my arm, which not only was bleeding but also had swollen. The policeman told me he was going to caution me and asked me if the injuries to my arm had been caused by my husband, adding that if I said yes, they would arrest Robert and charge him with domestic violence. In the morning, he would be in court on charges for domestic violence that carried a six-month mandatory sentence. I would not be allowed to drop the charges as it would be the police bringing the charges, not me. So after the caution, when the police asked me if my injuries had been caused by Robert, I said no. And they let him go. That made the second time they had been called out. I could not work for some days as my arm was badly swollen.

One day Craig found me. He had gotten my number from Karen. I had given him Karen's number at some point, so he had used it to call her to find me. I started to communicate with him regularly. He even told me he loved me. Things were looking up for us. He even sent me a photograph of himself with a card saying he loved me. And whenever I called him, the way he spoke to me made me feel emotionally strong and not bothered by the things Robert was doing to me.

I was making money and was able to maintain

myself. I had good friends and I was enjoying life, eating out, and arranging events for BEST. I worked on a couple of other record cover shoots as new record producers were setting up in Florida; this was before they all moved to Atlanta. I was also being encouraged to move my business to Atlanta. Now I wonder what the outcome of my life would have been if I had moved to Atlanta.

I've never seen cocaine even though it was all around. There was an abundance of disposable drug money where I lived and in surrounding counties. Working on my one-stop beauty spa concept, I identified two investors from Puerto Rico. The architect had finished the drawings, the business plan was finished, and the costing was being worked on. I was busy getting on with my life.

My business account was looking healthy, and my accountant suggested that I also file for my green card through employment. Even though I had been granted a work permit, my green card was taking a long time. Robert and I had been for an interview with immigration, but the immigration officer gave me a hard time and even threw my arrival card to Florida in the bin, saying I did not need it. I argued with him and took it out of the bin. I later found out that Robert knew him from the nightclub he worked at and had asked him to make life difficult for me.

I had no idea that Robert was calling the salon. If any of the male minders answered the phone, he was abusive to them and accused them of having sex with me.

Then during a call to Craig, just before Christmas 1988, out of the blue he said it was time I returned to England. I asked him if it was worth it for me to do so, if I had a chance with him. To my surprise, he said yes, adding that he was happy for us to talk about a future together. I was in shock. I could not believe what I was hearing. I was ready to give up everything to go back to England and start a life with Craig. *Could this really be happening to me?* I wondered. I was on cloud nine. I started dreaming and planning all the good things for my life with Craig.

It was now 1989, and I was calling Craig often. He was still making me feel good. Then one day the strangest thing happened. Leroy normally allowed me to use the phone in his office at the back of the salon to make my calls to England. I went to use the phone and knocked on the office door. I did not wait for him to say come in; I just pushed the door open. And there in front of me was the most handsome man. My heart jumped out of my chest. I felt as if I had known him all my life. He looked right into my soul, and we both knew we had found each other. His face lit up with the most beautiful smile. I closed the door so quickly that I just about heard Leroy saying, "I can come back later."

I ran out of the salon into the sunshine. I can't remember how far I walked before I stopped to breathe. My heart knew this man from a past life; he was not a stranger, but who was he to me?

By the time I got back to the salon, he was gone. For the rest of that day, I was weak. I did not see him again till one day at the end of March. I was in a cheque-cashing shop, where you can cash your cheques, buy stamps and money orders, and do other kinds of transaction. I was waiting in line to get served when I heard this voice. I did not look around to see who it was as I just knew it was him, even though on the day I had seen him in the salon office, I hadn't heard his voice. My legs started shaking. From where I was in the queue to the place where I'd be served, I would have to pass him. As I walked past him, I kept my eyes straight ahead, just using my side vision. I saw him raise his eyebrows at me slightly. Then I caught sight of the girl he was with and recognised her as a client. Now not only were my legs shaking, but also my heart was beating incredibly loudly. How I managed to keep myself composed to walk past him was a miracle.

I later learned his name was Kirk, and what was interesting was the conversation he was having with the girl, who was his son's mother. I established that both Kirk and Craig were born in April, as the conversation he was having with his son's mother was about the plans he had for his birthday at the end of the week.

Four weeks after my encounter with Kirk, I had spent a good part of the day at a shipping company at the airport, sending a bike to my son in England. I had to ask Robert to help me take the bike to the shipping company, and as usual, he was being a total idiot. It was one of those really hot days, and his car had no air conditioner. My intention was to take a nap as soon as I got home. About two hours after getting home and relaxing, my phone rang. It was Leroy's mother, telling me she had booked an appointment for me. I told her I was taking the rest of the day off, but she insisted that I had to do this appointment for her as a favour. The client was an important person, whom she would call to say I was on my way. She pushed, and I agreed.

When I got to the salon, it was busy and in full

swing. I went to my room and prepared for the facial appointment. Leroy's mother knocked on my door and, in her southern voice, said, "Your appointment is here, baby girl." I was in no hurry to get this appointment, but I put a smile on my face. As I walked towards the reception area, I saw the most well-pressed trousers and a pair of socks that matched beautiful shoes. To my surprise, they belonged to Kirk, the man who had set my heart beating. This time I could not run. He gave me the most incredible smile as if to say, *Yes, it's really me*. By the time we both had composed ourselves, I could hear Leroy's mother say, "This is your appointment, baby girl."

I walked in the direction of my facial room with him following me. As I got to my door, I saw that he had stopped to talk to most of the women getting their hair done. He seemed to be a very popular. It gave me more time to compose myself.

I am not sure how long I waited for him, but by the time he made it to my room, I was composed and had just about settled down. Then my facial room door was pushed open, and one of my clients, who was getting her hair done, came in. She seemed to know Kirk very well. She asked him why he had not called her, and he seemed to avoid her questions. It was obvious they had been in a relationship and that she did not know why it was over. He was making all kinds of excuses that just did not make sense. By the time she left, I knew more about him: he had a son, owned a few laundry businesses, and was building his house.

We talked after she left. I told him I was from England and that I would love to have my own spa. But most of all, he was enjoying the facial. He left after the facial and I was not sure how I felt.

The second facial appointment was almost the same. He called at the last minute. It was another one of those days when I was resting at home. He told Leroy's mother that he would come and pick me up from my house. She must have told him that I did not drive. Of course, I said no. At the end of the appointment, he gave me his business card. It had all his business numbers and his beeper number. He wrote his home number on it and said if ever I needed him for any reason, day or night, to just use his numbers. I took the card and wondered, *Why would this man think I would need him?*

Then one day he called me and said he was going out of town on a trip and would see me when he got back. He added that if I were to have any problems, I should call him on his beeper. I am not sure how long he was away, but as I got to the salon early one morning, I saw his car parked outside. As I got closer to the car, I saw one single battery-operated red rose in the back window. Somehow I knew the rose was for me. He said he would call me for a facial appointment, but he left without giving me the rose. I can't remember exactly how the meeting went, but I felt he had gotten cold feet as that rose was the words to declare his feelings for me. I didn't hear from him again for a long time.

Life with Robert was becoming more impossible. I spotted him following me a couple of times. One day he threw my clothes over the balcony of the apartment where we lived. So I decided to pack all my clothes into my suitcase and told him next time he could just throw the suitcase out. Then there was another time, I can't remember exactly what happened, but I had to stay the night at Karen's as there was some issue with Robert. When I arrived at work the next morning, I found that he had been by and had left my suitcase outside the salon. Luckily, Leroy's mother was already at the salon as he was leaving my suitcase by the salon door, and she was able to establish he was my husband. So when I got to work, she told me she had put my suitcase in my room. He was beginning to wear me down. I did not know the extent of his stalking me.

One day I was at the salon, but I was not busy. I felt frustrated that my plans were not coming together quickly enough. I was frustrated at staying in a marriage just for a green card because it was killing my passion. In my frustration, I went outside to sit on the wall. What happened next was not in my plans.

Kirk walked towards me with his brother, whom I had met a couple of times. In the beginning, Kirk would send him to pick up the towels I used during my facials to wash them for me as he knew I had to walk across the road in the hot sun to the laundry. He got his brother to pick up my towels twice a week, but his brother did it only a few times and then stopped. I also found out some years later that his brother had told him that I liked him.

As Kirk approached me, his brother kept his distance. I was so happy to see Kirk. He gave me the biggest smile and said, "I know that what I am feeling, you're feeling too. We need to meet and just talk it through. We don't have to act on anything." He knew I was married but wanted to help me get the things I needed to succeed as he could make it all happen. We had talked about my dream of a one-stop beauty spa, and he had been the one who invested start-up money for Tender Heart Salon, so we arranged to meet that afternoon at two o'clock. He walked with his brother into the shooting range shop next door to the salon.

Then out of the blue, Robert popped up and started his show, jumping up and down like a madman. He was saying he knew I had a man. The dirtiest words were coming out of his mouth. He was so loud that all the women who worked in the salon and the clients came out to see what was going on. I just blended into the crowd, watching him. Then Lora, my hairdressing girlfriend, asked, "Isn't that your husband?"

I answered, "No, girl. I don't know who that man is." He finally got in his car. I knew exactly what he was going to do. I called Karen. Luckily for me, she was off work, so I asked her to come and pick me up. I knew Robert had gone to get my suitcase to disgrace me.

As I waited for him to return, Kirk and his brother came out of the shooting range shop. Kirk asked me if I was OK as his brother had told him that while he was talking to me, there was a man looking at us very angrily. I told him, "Yes, it was my husband, and now he's gone home to get my clothes to throw me out." He said he would wait for him to come back.

Kirk and his brother sat in his big black Bronco and waited for Robert. As Robert pulled up, so did Karen. She pulled in right beside him and started screaming at him. He jumped out of his car to get my suitcase. He was in such a rage he did not see Kirk get out of his Bronco, stand tall, and pull up his trousers. Then he walked over to Robert, who was just about to throw my suitcase across the car park, not realising that Kirk was standing behind him. In a deep voice

Kirk told him, "Put the lady's suitcase down carefully, and get back in your car. Whatever misery you're in today, I will gladly put you out of it."

Robert slowly put the suitcase down and Karen picked it up and put it in her car. Robert quickly got back in his car and fled for his life. Kirk asked if I had somewhere to stay and said that he would follow me and Karen back to the apartment to make sure I had everything.

By the time I went into the salon to get my handbag, Lora was working on a client of ours. I told them what had happened, and straightaway, things were taken out of my hands. The client insisted that I move into her house and pay rent.

It would be safer for me as Robert would not know where I lived. Karen and I drove to the apartment, with Kirk following us to make sure that I had all my belongings, and then he left. He and I never kept the date for that afternoon. That was the last time I saw him for a while.

In the following weeks, Robert stalked me day and night. I had to use the shop's security boys to escort me out of the salon from the back door into their car. Then I lay on the back seat and they took me home. At night Robert was busy stalking all my friends' houses. I could not take the bus; I had to take a cab or get someone to come and pick me up. In the United States, when you move, you can choose to keep your phone number. I kept the phone number I had had at the apartment as it was in my name. I needed it as it was important so my family in England could contact me. Robert would not stop ringing the phone after I got home from work.

Then out of the blue, Craig called me and said he

was going to book a ticket for me to come to England
so we could talk about getting married. I decided
to take him up on it and asked my sister-in-law to
send me a telegram saying that my son was sick and
needed me. I went down to the immigration office
and got them to stamp my passport to leave the
United States for two weeks.

I got a call from Craig to say my ticket to England
was booked. He asked me to buy him a multimedia
video player, saying he would give me the money
when I got to England. There was no reason for me
not to believe he would give me the money back; after
all, he was a wealthy man.

I left Florida on a Friday and arrived in England
on Saturday morning. Craig was not at the airport
to meet me. I called him, and he asked me to get a
cab, saying that he would pay for it when I got to
the shop. I was so looking forward to seeing him,
and my heart was beating very fast. This was not a
dream. This was the man I loved sending for me to
come home to him. And after what I had been going
through in Florida, this was my dream becoming my
reality.

Everything in England looked very small. Even at
my short height, I felt like a giant. When I finally got
to Craig's shop, I was hoping he would take me in his
arms passionately. After all, I was looking fabulous.
My haircut was on point, my skin was glowing, my
clothes were just right, and my body was sexy.

But this man just smiled and started asking me
about my flight. He talked about all kinds of things.
There was no kiss, no contact. He wanted me to
accompany some girl on my return to the United
States. He asked me when I was going back. When

I told him I was staying for two weeks, he was not happy with me and said I had spoiled his plans. He talked about a new friend who was going to come by to see him. When this friend arrived, I could see he had gay tendencies. But he was a married man with a new baby. This friend was very pretty, and there was a sexual vibe between him and Craig.

By the time we were on our way to Craig's house, his attitude towards me had changed to one of hostility. He did not want to talk to me. And when we finally got to bed, he had problems making love to me. I allowed him to make all the moves. He switched on a video that was already set up to play a porn movie. He needed to hear the moaning and sex talk in the movie to help him with his sexual issues. I now knew my suspicion about his sexuality was right. I'd always known he struggled with his sexuality and was hiding it, but if only he knew it did not matter to me as I already loved him.

By the time I woke up on Sunday morning from being jet-lagged, Craig was already up and ready to go out. He did not want to talk to me; he wanted to leave me in the house on my own. I managed to get ready quickly and got in the car with him. He was even more upset with me for coming with him. He just drove around, not doing anything special, not going anywhere to see anyone. It was obvious that I had upset his plans and that he was not able to see who he had planned to be with, with me there. The only place he stopped off at was at his younger brother's house. It was nice to see his brother as we got on well.

When we got back to Craig's house, he started shouting at me. He just about managed to cook me some food that I did not like. When I tried to ask why he had sent for me, he began showing off how much money he had, saying that if we were to get married, I would have to sign a prenuptial agreement. I agreed and said that I would be happy to sign one. Then he brought up some other excuse. Every time he put up a challenge regarding getting married, I agreed to whatever he was asking. Then he said to me, "You're not the kind of woman I want to be married to."

I was devastated. We managed to get through the night. On Monday morning, I went into work with him. It was the longest Monday. Things just got worse; he would not talk to me. It was the same on Tuesday. And on Wednesday morning, he said it was best that I left. This was a dangerous move for me as he had only bought me a one-way ticket and did not pay me for the video recorder. I did not know the extent of his spitefulness.

It was a big surprise for my son when I turned up without warning. I called Craig every day to see if he had gotten a return ticket for me. He was being very difficult. So I cut my visit with my son short and returned to the city, where I stayed with my girlfriend Janet, whom I had worked with on her fashion shows several times. She now had her collection in lots of outlets.

I went to Craig's shop and he directed me to his travel agent around the corner. Luckily, it was just around the corner from his shop. When I tried to book my flight, all direct flights to Florida were booked. Virgin Atlantic had just started flying, and the flights were ninety-nine pounds one way to the United States. So I got a flight to New York instead. The agent said they would have a ticket ready for me when I got to New York to connect to Florida, adding that when I got there, I should go to the information desk to get my ticket to Florida. But when I got to New York, there was no ticket waiting for me. I called Craig. It was late in England when he answered. When he heard my voice, he put the phone down. Luckily for me, my eldest brother was living in New York with his family, so I spent the night with them. I wrote my brother a cheque, and he gave me the cash so I could pay for my ticket back to Florida.

During my stay in England with Janet, we talked about my coming back to England and using the first-floor space at her fashion studio to set up my skincare business. I was giving it a lot of thought. I was not sure I could give up my business in Florida and return to England.

When I got back to Florida, I decided to call Kirk. It was time to dump Craig, and as for Robert, I was not going back to him, green card or no green card. When I called Kirk's home number, some woman answered the phone, so I put the phone down. She called back and asked me if someone from my number had called, and I said no. That was the end of that. He had a woman, or so I thought, not knowing at the time that it was his sister.

Even after the two weeks away, Robert did not calm down. I did not have the money to keep taking cabs, and I could not keep calling my friends to come and pick me up. Robert was waiting at bus stops and circling around the area he thought I would be living in. I always managed to spot him before he could see me, so I would hide in a shop or just take cover where I could. One morning as I was about to leave the house, I opened the front door and saw Robert just in time to pull back inside. He now had gotten closer to where I was living. Then one morning I came out of my street onto the busy main road, and there was Robert. He got out of his car, grabbed me, and tried to pull me into his car. I started fighting him, and we fell to the ground. As I fell, my blouse got caught on a wire fence and ripped. In those days, I did not wear a bra. It was a wrap blouse, so I was naked on top. My skirt was also a wrap style. We were on the ground rolling around. Luckily, two young white boys stopped their car and came to my rescue. They got Robert off me and held him back, and I managed to get a few kicks into him. When they let him go, he ran off to his car and sped away. I had to knock on someone's door to call the police and a friend. When the police arrived, they were very familiar with my domestic violence as this was the third time they had been called out. The police were not going to leave it at that this time. I had to go down to the courthouse and file charges and get a restraining order. I had been contemplating returning to England and after coming out of the courthouse and making charges against Robert, I decided to pack up and return to England.

I started winding down my business and making arrangements to return to England. My plan was to rent the ground floor of Janet's studio and start my new skincare business in the city.

Chapter 11
Finding My Purpose

It was 1990, and my plans were in place. I was packed, my flight was booked, and the shippers had been booked to pick up my machine and bed that I used for my facial treatments. The week before I was due to leave, one of my clients made an appointment for me to do her make-up. It was the same client who had come into my room when Kirk was having his first facial appointment with me. She was getting married that afternoon, so I asked her if she was getting married to Kirk. She said no and asked if I had not heard that he was in jail. After the shock, I asked her what for. She would not say, but she went on to mention that he had been in jail before. She had supported him while he was there, and never heard from him when he got out of jail. The first time she had seen him after his release was when he was having his facial appointment. When he came home from jail, he just turned his back on her as if their relationship had never happened.

After she left, I got the card that he had given me and called one of his business numbers. When his brother answered the phone, I asked him if he could get Kirk to call me as I was leaving the United States for good. About ten minutes later, I had a call from Kirk. I told him I was leaving the United States, and we exchanged addresses. He did not tell me why he was in jail, and I never asked.

On Monday morning, the shippers arrived at Tender Heart to collect my equipment. They took everything except my facial steamer. When I turned up at the salon to see what was going on, Leroy's mother would not allow them to take the steamer, claiming that it belonged to the salon. Leroy was in jail, and she was running the business. I had to call the police and produce the receipt for the steamer. When I got it home, I decided to test the steamer to see if it was damaged. I plugged it in, and it blew me across the room. The plug sparked a fire, and I had to quickly pull the cord out of the outlet. Some years later, I found out that Leroy's mother was a Freemason. One day I had had some photographs taken and was showing them around the salon.

I found it weird that she insisted I give her one. She had also managed to get a photo of Lora. For some reason, Lora had to go to her house, where she found both our pictures on an altar Leroy's mother had in her house. This was to hurt us. Her last words to me when I left Tender Heart was that I would never be successful.

I left Florida on a Friday night flight. As I looked down on Florida, I said I needed to find the key to life. I had plenty of tears in my eyes as I had made a real home in Florida and was now leaving without fulfilment of my son's dream.

Back in England I was trying to settle in the city and staying with Janet. I had planned to rent space from her in her studio to set up my skincare business. Of course, I did not understand it then, but she knew I was emotionally vulnerable. She had encouraged me to come back to England for her own good. She was in trouble with her business and was having problems paying her rent, so it suited her purposes for me to sublet from her. She was constantly in and out of court with the landlord and was lucky that the judge always ruled in her favour. Roger had advised me not to rent the space from her, but I was already committed. I was staying at her house, but she soon quickly moved me on. I was glad of that as her adolescent daughter stole all my jewellery. Janet arranged for me to rent a room from one of her girlfriends. That did not last long as the girlfriend was not child-friendly. So the lady who did the sewing at Janet's studio said I could move into her house. My son quickly fitted into life with me; we started out with him staying with me on weekends.

On my return to England, I found out Craig was not in the country and would be away for three months in Africa, where he was building a department store. Little did I know he had plans to return to Africa to live. I was still very much in love with him and had decided before I came back to England that I would try to get pregnant by him. If he had not been in Africa on my return, I would have had a child with him. I felt this was the way to stop loving him and give the love I had for him to his child. At least that was my plan. I really did not think it through properly as it really was not going to be the best choice for me. I had stopped taking the pill before I left Florida, so I stood a better chance of getting pregnant by him.

When I got back to England, I visited my hometown on the first week and contacted Leon. He immediately arranged for me to spend an afternoon with him having lunch. He also booked a hotel room not far from his office for us to have sex. This threw a spanner in the works as he was not the one I wanted to get me pregnant. But he did. When I told Leon I was pregnant, he was happy for me to have the baby, but I did not want to keep the baby. He arranged an appointment for me in a beautiful private clinic in my hometown to have an abortion. I've never regretted it as, at the time, becoming pregnant was a bad choice.

About a week after I had the abortion, Craig returned to England. When I called him, he was shocked to hear my voice. He asked me where I was, and when I told him I was in the city, he could not believe it. He asked me to come by and to see him, which I did, but I took my son with me. My son never liked Craig. Craig soon left to go back to Africa to finish his shop. It was that day that he told me his intention was to return to Africa to live. He was away for three months. By the time he returned, I had set up my skincare business.

When Craig returned, he called me, and I went to see him. The weakness I had, a result of my love for him, took over and I slept with him that night. He had bought me a beautiful African outfit.

Then he went off again to Africa for another three months. While he was away, a young lady walked into my clinic. She was also from Africa. Straightaway, Nina and I hit it off and became friends. She was also a single mother. She had a daughter who was around five. We started spending time together.

My son started secondary school in the area where I had set up my business. He was such a happy, friendly boy and very helpful to me. He was like a husband, doing all my errands, such as shopping and laundry. He knew how to make money doing jobs for people. He got a job at the corner shop, cleaning the stockroom. Then he had his paper round. He also did errands for the staff who worked in the salon. He never stopped working.

My business was going well. I did an editorial in my old magazine *Black Hair and Beauty* and for the *Jamaican Gleaner* newspaper. That quickly built up my clientele. I employed one person, and rent was paid on time.

I got my divorce from Robert. He still had to go to court to answer to the charges of assault. The judge told him the only reason why he was not going to jail was because I had returned to England. The judge gave me up to seven years to claim my green card. If I had been in court, he would have given it to me there and then.

I made contact with Kirk. He was still in jail.

I truly believe that nothing in life is a coincidence. The universe hears our cries and brings us the perfect plan into our experiences, and the perfect plan came together for me.

I attended a beauty exhibition, and as I was walking around, I heard a man calling my name. I was approached by a white man who asked, "You don't remember me?" I kept looking at him but had no idea who he was. He told me he used to be my sales representative when I worked as a beauty consultant for Lentheric, Morny, and Cyclax. I would never have recognised him as he had changed. He told me that he had survived on my sales to look after his family and that after I had left, he lost his house and his wife left him as he was not getting the big commission from my sales. Of course, I was in shock. Then he told me that Lentheric, Morny, and Cyclax was at the exhibition and that my former supervisor (I won't repeat what he called her) was working on the exhibition. What an opportunity for me to thank this lady for sacking me and changing my life for the good.

I made my way to the Lentheric, Morny, and Cyclax stand, but she was not there. The new owner of the company told me that she would not be working on the stand till the next day. I knew I would not be able to come back the next day, so I asked him if he would make sure to give her a message for me. He said he would. I told him to tell her, "Thanks for allowing me to experience travelling all over England and the world. I became a top make-up artist for television, magazines, fashion and beauty shows. I also got my qualification as a beauty therapist and no longer need to read the instructions from the back of a box. I have had a skincare business in Florida and now have one in the city, and I have met some of the richest men, who have allowed me to experience the good life." He looked at me strangely as I gave him the message. I told him I used to work for his company when it was at its best. He said he would remember my message and deliver it to my former supervisor.

I also visited the department store in my hometown and caught up with Jeana, who had caused me to get the sack. When I told her of my accomplishments, she was honest with me and said she had made some bad choices. She had given her life to a job that had left her a lonely old woman with no husband or children. She had never travelled outside our hometown and had nothing to look forward to. She would gladly trade with me in what I had achieved for myself.

Things were going smoothly for me, and then one

weekend we had a great deal of snow. It started on Friday, and by Saturday, it had gotten worse. I had forgotten what freezing cold can do to the plumbing system. I left my business early on Saturday evening, and when I got back to work on Monday morning, the whole first-floor ceiling had collapsed into my section. The landlord's son cursed me for having been foolish not to switch off the main water pipe to stop the water from freezing in the pipe. Luckily for me, I had insurance separate from their building insurance.

I no sooner got over that when the following week, again on Friday, two musclemen turned up with a court order for me to vacate the premises. I was in shock. They allowed me one hour to collect as much as I could. Luckily, I had made friends with a builder who was working on a property a few doors away. I asked him to help me move the essential things that I would need to work. When I called Janet, she already knew it was going to happen. I went to see her solicitor, who told me how to get back into the premises legally. He said I should call the police to notify them of my intentions, which I did. They told me they would delay the response if they got a call about the premises.

So I made arrangements to go back to the premises and get the rest of my belongings. I did this with the help of my eleven-year-old son and his photographic memory. He walked by the shop and looked at the padlock. We went to a padlock shop, and my son identified the padlock that they had on the shop door. The builder whom I had befriended agreed to help me; he would move the rest of my belongings into the premises he was working on.

I was angry with Janet for having put me in this

position. I did not tell her what I was planning to do, but the lady whose house my son and I were living in had told her. So Sunday morning, when I turned up to enter the premises, Janet turned up with a big truck and a crew of people to remove her belongings. I called a locksmith to get the padlock off, and in less than an hour, the builder had cleared my belongings out of the premises.

But Janet was taking her time as she had a lot of things to clear. What she should have done was just to remove her belongings and put them on the other side of the road. Then they could take their time to pack the truck. The landlord had his shop next door, and he turned up and called the police before Janet had finished clearing out her belongings. As promised, the police took their time. By the time the police arrived on foot, everything had been cleared out, and the same padlock was replaced on the door. So when the police and the landlord checked to see if there was a break-in, they found no sign of one. I have not seen Janet since that day, but I heard that she went into teaching fashion at a college.

Craig had been away on one of his three-month trips to Africa. I was surprised when he came back. I called him, and he invited me to come to his house for dinner. Of course, he expected me to stay the night, but I had made up my mind that I was going to detach my emotions from him. I had taken a taxi from the train station to his house and had asked the taxi driver to come back for me at a certain time.

When I got to his house, Craig looked at me funny as I did not have my overnight bag with me, but he did not say anything. We had dinner, and he finally asked me if I was not intending to stay the night.

I told him I had a very early appointment in the morning and that staying the night would make me late. I had made up my mind that I was not going to sleep with him.

But he wanted to have sex, so we went to the bedroom. He took his clothes off and lay on the bed. I had to dig deep to say no to him. I told him he had to meet me halfway before I would have sex with him again. He was in shock that I would say that to him. There he was with an erection, and me saying no. He told me to get out of his house. I called the cab company and was told that the taxi man was waiting for me outside. It was a good thing I had made this plan as Craig was happy for me to be on the street late at night because his pride was hurt. Rejected, I cried all the way home in the back of the taxi. The driver tried his best to speak words of comfort to me. I was in pain, but it had to be done.

My son and I moved in with Nina and her daughter. Nina and I were both single. She worked nights, and I worked days and her place was closer to my son's school, so it was convenient. I had set up my skincare business one street away from the old premises, above the Timeless Hair and Beauty Salon. It was in the room where I had had my first interview with Mrs Marley of Hollywood Curls.

I still had pain from all the love I had for Craig. One Sunday I decided to turn up at his house with some of the skincare products that he was interested in buying from me. We had not spoken since the night I had said no to having sex with him. When I got to the top of his street, I saw him using the public telephone. He pretended he did not see me, so I went to his house and waited for him. His beautiful red Mercedes convertible sports car was parked outside his house with the top down. He came down the street, jumped in his car, and drove off. He returned angrily, asking why I had come to his house uninvited. I followed him into the house but did not stay long as he asked me to leave. He slammed the door behind me so hard, it was as if my heart had smashed into pieces. I stood on the steps of his house with pain in my heart. I looked at his red car and thought, *He loves his car more than he loves me*. I wanted to hurt his car. To think that I had allowed this man to treat me this way! This love that I had for him had to die. As I sat on the train going home, the tears were just rolling down my cheeks.

A black man in a yellow-yoke jumper came and sat beside me. He opened a newspaper that he stretched out in front of us. I could feel myself leaning on his shoulder. It felt as if his arms were around me as he said, "There, there, there." When he got off at his stop, he stood on the platform looking at me with loving eyes as the train pulled away.

The next day, out of the blue Kirk called me and said he wanted to have a relationship with me. I took all the love I had for Craig and gave it to Kirk. A few weeks later, Craig turned up at my business to tell me he was going to live in Africa and would come back to England every six months to do his exports. I was cold towards him and could not understand why he had come to say goodbye.

My son and I had to move again as the living arrangements with Nina were not working out. My son started complaining that he still wanted to go live in the United States. I became good friends with Anne, one of my clients. She was like a long-lost daughter to me. With her support, I was able to leave my son and make my first trip back to Florida since returning to England. Back in Florida, I got my business back up and running, and my clients were happy. Lora had established her own hair salon and put together a beautiful facial room from which I could run my business. Karen had bought her own house and had split from her husband, so as two single mothers, we were able to support each other. When my son moved to Florida, I settled him in school.

My new routine was to spend two weeks in Florida and two weeks in England. I still had one young lady working for me in England.

While I was in Florida, I started visiting Kirk in prison. On my second visit, I learned they had moved him to a facility in Georgia. It was going to be difficult to travel to visit him in Georgia. When he was local, I could get a friend or taxi to take me to the facility.

Kirk arranged for me to visit him with his family. I went to his house and met his mother and her husband. The husband was a nice man who looked like my father. Kirk's sister and her daughter had moved into his house. His mother was a very controlling and aggressive woman.

He had arranged for me to stay with them at his house so I could travel with them to visit him. I knew straightaway that they did not really like me. They had no class about them and saw me as a threat.

I travelled with them by car to Georgia. We left at one in the morning. The journey was long, and the highway had no lights. As we drove through the night, there were hardly any other cars on the road. From time to time, a car passed on the opposite side of the road, and that was as much light as we got. It was the scariest journey I had ever made—both going and returning.

When we finally got to Georgia, we checked into a local hotel to shower and change. The plan was to stay the night and then, after visiting Kirk the next day, start driving back to Florida. The only things we could carry into the prison were money and identification, all in a see-through holder.

All inmates wore the same uniforms, but what they did was to make the uniform look like a designer outfit—clean, well ironed, and sharp. I had no problems falling in love with Kirk. He and his family were like chalk and cheese given the way he looked and talked. They were more like a hillbilly family.

After we visited him, we started to make our way back to Florida. Just outside the city boundary, the car broke down. All that surrounded us were trees and swamps, no lights. Daylight had just fallen into darkness, and we did not know what to do. Georgia was still a dangerous place for black people. It was deep slavery country, and they were still calling black men "boys". So there we were, stuck on a redneck slavery road in the pitch of darkness, with one gun among all of us. If we were to elect two people to walk back to the town to get help, they would have to take the gun, and then the ones who stayed in the car would be without a gun. And how could we decide who would go and who would stay?

A few cars passed us going into the city, but no one stopped to help us. We decided we would all stay in the car for the night. This really was quite dangerous. As time went by, we saw no more cars going into the city. Maybe it was my imagination in the blackness of the night, but I could hear the cries of the slaves. I could feel their spirits. It was as if they were hanging from the trees around us.

Then, as we all huddled in the car, a big beam of light shone into the car. An army truck pulled up behind us, and we waited. A white man dressed in an army uniform knocked on the car window. Kirk's stepfather rolled the window down. The white man said, "Hi, folks. You broken down?" He said he would help us, but he did not have the space for all of us in the army truck, so he would take one of us with him and bring a van back to pick us all up and take us back to the hotel. This required a lot of trust. We decided that the stepfather should go with him. We would keep the gun. They went off, and in less than an hour, they were back.

We stayed another night at the hotel. The white man came back in the morning and towed the car to the local garage. They did not have the necessary part in stock, so we had to hire a U-Haul van. We hitched the car to the van, and we all squashed into the van. But before we left, the white man told us why he had helped us. Apparently his wife had gotten lost in a black neighbourhood and two black men had rescued her, booked her into a hotel, called him, and stayed with her till he came and got her. He promised himself that one day he would repay a black person or persons for those two black men's kindness, and we were the lucky ones.

When we got back to Florida, I had a feeling that Kirk's family did not want to see me again after that trip. But on my next visit to Florida, I went to say hello to them, just out of respect. Kirk's mother came to the door with a long shotgun pointed at me and Karen. She told us to clear off and not come back. I never did see them again. I can't remember what excuse Kirk gave me to defend his mother's behaviour, but I do remember him saying his mother always got rid of his girlfriends.

My son settled into school and quickly adapted to American life. He loved it. He was a teenager by then. The US school system is different from England's, and the age for high school in the United States is fifteen. My son had already been in high school when he was in England, so they could not fit him back into junior high school. He was placed in high school with young people between the ages of fifteen and nineteen. My son never told any of his friends that he was much younger than they. Everything seemed to work out in his favour, as if it was just meant to be.

We both settled into a new way of life. I worked hard growing my skincare business in England and writing a beauty column for *Black Hair and Beauty* magazine.

On my visit to the United States every month, I took three days out and visited Kirk, travelling for fifteen hours on the Greyhound bus to Georgia by myself. He asked me to marry him, and I tried to encourage him to agree we would get married while he was inside so as not to waste my time.

He was looking at spending twelve years in prison, and I wanted some commitment to wait all those years for him. I was concerned he would come home and decide I was not right for him. He made all kinds of excuses not to marry me while he was inside. I let it go, but in my heart, it was not sitting well.

During these periods, I saw Robert, and we became good friends. He and Lora had also become good friends. We had secret sex. It was good as I made it all about me. I even got him to take me shopping, and he bought me quite a few pieces of clothing.

Life became a routine for five years. I had had far more friends and things to do in Florida, whereas living in England, I had very few friends. And since Jamaica was only one hour fifteen minutes from Florida, I could make quick visits to see my parents.

The age for starting to drive in the United States is fifteen. My son started pressuring me to buy him a car, but I felt I had to grieve him first before I got him a car. He had a friend who lived on the same street whose parents had bought him a big Jeep. I told my son that under no circumstances should he ride with this friend. His friend was always driving fast and showing off.

I did buy my son a car, but I kept it in the drive for three months. During my grieving process, I imagined him in a coffin, burying him in a grave, and walking away. But on one of my visits, I decided to pay the taxes and insure the car for my son. On the day I was returning to England, he drove me to the airport in his car, along with his best friend.

As he drove me to the airport, I was not feeling well in my heart. They dropped me off and left. My flight was delayed for about three hours. I tried calling the house, but no one was in.

By the time I got back to England, I just knew I would get a call that would grieve me. After I got into work, I indeed got the phone call that my son had been in an accident, but it was not in his car. The story was that he had driven to the mall after dropping me off at the airport. Going to the local shopping centre had gone OK, but on his way out of the car park, his car was hit and totalled right off. Neither he nor his best friend was injured. Nor was the passenger of the car that hit him, who happened to be a doctor.

After that was sorted out, he went with his best friend to his house. Some of their other friends, including the boy with the big Jeep, happened to be there, and my son decided to get a ride home with him. On their way home, the boy drove on a yellow light, and a big truck slammed into the passenger side of the Jeep. My son almost lost his eyes. His femur was broken in three places and splintered. The other boy came out without a scratch.

I called my son in hospital and caught up with him just as he was on his way into surgery. I told him I was not going to return to Florida until I was due back in two weeks, and that he had to man up. If he were to decide to do something that I had told him not to do, he would have to deal with the consequences. He was much older than I was when I'd had to walk my journey by myself. But my son was not alone. He is the kind of person who makes friends and is loved by all who know him. His girlfriend at the time was our neighbour. Her mother was single and was a very loving mother. She took my son and his best friend under her wing. He had built a network of adopted family, so I was not worried, but it still did not make up for my not being there. But I knew with good communication and being prepared to listen to him when he was ready to unload his emotions on me would make him a better man, father, and individual in the future.

This was not the only problem that I had with my son. He was failing in school and should have had better grades as he was two years ahead with the start he had coming from England. He stopped working on his grades. And then time caught up with him. He was going to be eighteen and should have been graduating from high school. I received a letter from the school to go and see his head of year to sign forms for him to leave school and attend some adult education programme where they sent all students who were failing high school.

When I got to the meeting, I told the head of year I was not going to allow my son to be uprooted and put into an environment with other young people who had no dreams and had lost their way. My son had wanted to be an aviator since he was young, and I had to keep his dream alive. The head of year was really disappointed that I was not cooperating with the process. He was condescending and said he felt as if he were a doctor who had just told me I had a few days to live, but I was refusing to take the treatment and was willing to die. I said to him that my son had been failing for a long time, and if they were really interested, they should have brought it to my attention sooner. I told him I loved my son, and I forgave the head of year for wanting my son to fail, but I said that my son would stay at the school as long as it took him to graduate. I am sure the head of year was thinking I was a crazy woman, but I was not afraid of their system.

My son, very proud of the way I had defended him, made up his mind to refocus on his dream and did after-school catch up. A few months later, his head-of-year teacher had a massive heart attack and, on his return to school, was put on soft duties in the office to work out the time until his pension. My son made all the grades, got back on track and graduated with his class. He was accepted to an aviation college.

I felt I was changing spiritually. As I made more and more visits to Georgia to see Kirk, I was having deep dreams that felt real, and the connection to Georgia was growing stronger. Call it déjà vu, but deep down in my heart, Georgia was not an unfamiliar place to me. At the time, there were not many hotels in the town, and the one I chose to stay at seemed to hold some past memory for me. I normally stayed on the first floor on the side of the hotel, but on one visit, they put me in a room on the ground floor.

During the night, I had one of those real dreams. In the dream I was being prepared for a special ceremony. A Turkish lady, who was my friend in England with a dress shop next to Timeless Hair Salon, was dressing me and rubbing me with some special cream. There were other ladies there, helping her. They took me to a special room where a Star of David was on the floor. An altar of fire was in the middle of the star. All the men in the room wore special robes. Other people were dressed in black and white for a ceremony to be performed on me. They drew blood from under my big toe on my left foot. There was a man stretched out naked on the floor. It was my school friend Campbell. I danced around him in a sexual way, and as I danced, my clothes were taken off me by the men dressed in their special robes. I lay on top of Campbell and performed sex. As I climaxed, I cut his throat and caught his blood in a silver cup. I took the blood over to the fire. But at that point, I woke up sweating. It felt as if it had all happened in the room I was sleeping in.

Another time, the local taxi picked me up after a visit to see Kirk. There were already two passengers in the taxi. The driver dropped off the first passenger. The other passenger was a black man. As the taxi approached the area where the black man lived, the energy of déjà vu was strong. It was the black neighbourhood of the old slave quarters. My heart almost jumped out of my chest. Deep in my heart, I knew I had known this place before this lifetime. Back in England, I had had a dream that I was in the house I had been born in, in Jamaica. I was looking out the same window in the sitting room in which I had seen my dead grandmother appear the night my mother was very angry with my eldest brother for getting home late. I saw my youngest brother running, and behind him was a handsome young man running too. My brother threw a package towards the window I was looking out of. I ran out and quickly picked up the package. Following behind the young man and my brother were the police, chasing them.

This dream, along with the one in Georgia, played on my mind, and spirituality rocked my awareness. I did not know that most of my clients in Florida all went to the same church, and I was already with my soul group. Karen was reading a book that was the biggest buzz at the time, a spiritual adventure book titled *The Celestine Prophecy*. One of my clients was talking about it to me as her church was holding workshops and studies on the book. The premise of the book was that in life, there is no coincidence. Karen was lent the book by her friend, and she wanted me to read the book before I returned to England in three days time.

The friend who had loaned Karen the book invited her to church. Karen and I talked about it and decided to go on Sunday as I did not have to be at the airport till the evening. On Saturday, the client who had told me about the workshop studies at her church saw the book on my workstation; I kept it there so as to read it every chance I had. She was so excited. "That's the book I've been telling you about, the one that my church is doing the workshops on!"

Then when my next client came, she said, "You are reading the book." I told her I had to try to finish reading it by that evening as I had to give it back to Karen. She told me I could buy my own copy at the airport and secretly left me some money for it on my workstation. I called to tell her that she had left some money, and she said it was for me to buy the book at the airport.

When Karen and I got to church on Sunday, to my surprise, most of my clients were there, including the one who had told me about the workshop and the one who had left the money for me to buy the book. Even my accountant and other people I knew were at the church. The teachings were what I had been looking for in a church. It was in line with what I believed in, and the minister, Mary Tompkin, was a dynamic teacher.

On my return to England the following morning, I was on the train reading the book, which I had purchased at the airport. A man next to me started talking to me about the book.

I had been on this spiritual journey all my life, as I believe that every human has a purpose, but we are not always conscious of this purpose. At this moment in time, my consciousness level was raised, and I realised I was not alone in my beliefs. I had found my soul group, and it was more expansive than I knew. The true consciousness of my self-discovery came to life for me. I found the true meaning of transformation. I was excited and wanted everyone to come along with me.

The next book that became my new Bible was *Conversations with God* by Neale Donald Walsh. I did not have to hide my beliefs, I was not going mad, and my self-confidence in my thoughts had reached a high level.

When I was in Florida, l went to church every Sunday. They always made a tape recording of the service, and I never left church without my tape so I could listen to the message over and over during the week, till I went back to church. The well of happiness inside me opened, and I was truly happy and growing spiritually. This awareness of consciousness within me was not really new. It had always been within me, waiting to be born. I started to remember my dreams. They were real and meaningful events showing me my past life story, my present, and the future. At first I could not work out the meaning of my dreams. I started writing down my dreams, so I had evidence of them as they came to pass. I was able to work out their meanings. I was enjoying living the best days of my life.

It was 1998, and my youngest brother was getting married in August. This would be a big family reunion with my parents, who were visiting England for the first time since they had gone home to Jamaica. My eldest brother and his family were also making the trip back to England from the United States. My parents travelled to Florida and got to see my son and where we lived and met Karen for the first time. Then we all travelled back to England together.

Chapter 12

The Man of My Dreams and the Journey to My Life's Purpose

August 1998, travelling back to England from Florida with my parents, was a very special time. It allowed me to have the experience with them that I should have had as a child, when I made the life-saving journey to England, sick, with some stranger who only cared because she was being paid. Both my parents were afraid of flying, whereas I love flying. On this trip I felt that I was the parent, and they were my children. As everyone on the flight settled down to sleep for the night, my father pulled his hat over his face and went to sleep, praying he would never show his emotions. My mother did not sleep. All night she watched the flight path of the aeroplane on the television. I held her hand, and she prayed all night, till the plane landed in England.

My brother collected our parents and drove them to our hometown. On Friday I made my way home to prepare with everyone for the wedding. My brother getting married was a miracle as he was a young man who liked to have fun. He was not short of women and children.

The day I arrived for my brother's wedding, I was looking and feeling my best. Everything went perfectly. It was a big wedding. My brother was well known in the community and had a big following as a local disc jockey.

It was a beautiful summer's day. Everyone looked beautiful. The reception was packed with friends and family. I was the one among my siblings elected to make a speech. This day, destiny turned up. "Your destiny doesn't just happen; it arrives." And on this day, the most powerful destiny of my life arrived at my brother's wedding reception. Everyone was greeting each other and finding their seats to settle down. I was just pulling my seat out to sit down, when I had the urge to look back. My eyes went straight to the entrance. Bouncing down the steps like the cutest, most lovable puppy was the sweetest chocolate boy. My heart jumped out of my chest and into his, and our hearts started to beat as one. He looked straight into my soul, and I into his. We were no strangers to each other.

He sat right behind me. My heart was racing very fast. All I wanted to do was to be in his arms, to have him holding me. I had never felt passion on fire like this. I could not breathe. At one point I got up to go to the toilet. I don't how I made it without my knees buckling. He did not take his eyes off me. I just about made it through my speech.

After dinner, when the speeches were over, it was time to hit the dance floor. Things were taking time to warm up, and my parents were still mingling with family and friends. We were all trying not to get into the dancing out of respect to my parents. At one point, I was standing between my mum and dad, and my chocolate boy came and said hello to them. He whispered to me, "How long are you going to keep me waiting?" Then he walked off.

As soon as my parents left, I went to find my chocolate boy. There he was, rolling a joint. I went

up to him, held his beautiful face in my hands, and said, "You're too beautiful and special to be smoking joints." I walked off to talk to someone, giving myself some more time to compose myself. But when I turned around to talk to him again, he was gone.
I looked everywhere for him, even in the car park. He was nowhere to be seen. At one point during the evening, I had seen him talking to one of my male cousins, so I asked him where my chocolate boy was. He told me he was gone. But at least my cousin told me his name and said that he was a good friend of my brother's, adding that if I needed to find him, I should ask my brother. My world came together in one moment and then fell apart the next.

When I got into bed that night, I cried and cried. I sank into despair. No one knew what was going on inside me. I felt as if the life had been sucked out of me. My heart was crying, and the tears would not stop. I was not brave enough to ask my brother for the chocolate boy's number, and somehow I felt my cousin was not going to take the responsibility to be the one to give me his number. Not even the loving letters and phone calls from Kirk could quench or put out the fire in my heart, deep down in my soul, for my chocolate boy. I kept asking God what was going on and to show me what this energy of madness was about. Who was this man who was consuming me? Why him? Why me?

Then one night I got my answer in a dream. I dreamed I was back in the slave quarters of Georgia. There was a long fence in a field, and sitting on the fence was a little boy who looked just like my chocolate boy. There was a man picking crops in the field, and he looked just like Kirk. I was also picking crops. The little boy was very happy. The sun was shining.

And then the moment changed. I looked up, and walking towards me were policemen. They came right at me, arrested me, and marched me away with them. I saw Kirk, who was my father, look up, but he kept working. And my baby chocolate boy, my son, was sitting on the fence with his arms outstretched, crying, "Please don't take my mummy away. Please don't go." I was taken to jail and locked up with many other women. I was being jailed for killing a man.

I woke up crying. My dream was quite clear to me. These were two men I loved. One was my father, and the other was my son from my past life story. And my past had caught up with me in my present life. That's why the energy was so consuming.

I was in wonderland for days. When I got brave and called my brother, I asked him to give my number to my chocolate boy. I did not hear anything from my chocolate boy, so I started calling my brother's house and talking to his wife. I asked about my chocolate boy. Sometimes I called but had just missed him as he was dropping by my brother's house very often. My sister-in-law said my brother would not give him my number as he was being protective of me. She told me that my chocolate boy visited their home almost every day. So, in October 1998, I called my brother's house, and my sister-in-law said my chocolate boy had invited them to his birthday party on Saturday. She suggested that I come home on Saturday night, go to his birthday party, and give him my number myself.

So the plan went into action. My friend Anne, who was the manager of a well-known car rental company, her new boyfriend, his brother, and I decided to drive to my hometown to go to the birthday party. My brother was shocked to see me turn up at his house. We stayed for a drink as it was too early to show up at the party.

When we got there, the party was packed, and my chocolate boy was nowhere to be seen, but we danced till midnight. Then, out of the blue, my chocolate boy walked in with a girl by his side. The possibility that he might have a woman never crossed my mind, but seeing him with one was not a challenge for me. He looked at me, but he seemed not fully sure it was me, as if he was shocked to see me. He played it cool and stood next to my brother.

At some point, I made my way to the toilet. I took my business card out of my bag and held it in the palm of my hands. As I walked back into the party, my brother was still talking to him. He quickly said to my chocolate boy, "This is my sister from the city."

The chocolate boy responded, "I knew it was you." I shook his hand and pressed my card into it. He took the card carefully, so no one would see the pass.

Soon after, as my mission was accomplished, my group and I decided to leave and drive back to the city. As I was leaving, my chocolate boy was positioned quite close to me. I turned to say goodbye to him and whispered to him to call me at five o'clock the next day. He said he would.

There was no stopping our hearts. I could not sleep that night as my adrenaline was high. Five o'clock Sunday could not come fast enough. I had to go to my business to take that phone call as I did not have a phone where I was living. I was there from four o'clock, and right at five o'clock, my chocolate boy called. His voice made every fibre of my body vibrate. The first thing I asked him was, "Do you think this is the first time we are having a life together?" He said no. I asked, "Who do you think I was to you in our previous life together?"

He said, "You were my mother, and this time you will never leave me."

I had made up my mind not to love him for the good things he was but for the bad things. So I asked him how many children he had, how many women he had, and how I would fit into his programme of women. I told him he should never lie to me—no matter how bad things were.

If we could have jumped through the phone to be with each other during that first phone call, we would have. We talked and talked. I told him about Kirk, and of course, he was cautious about telling me about himself. He was not sure if I was for real as I seemed far too easy.

We started talking several times a day. We talked about him coming down to the city to see me. We tried to arrange for him to come down when a girlfriend of mine was having a party, but she had to cancel it at the last minute. So we made arrangements for him to come down on a Sunday. I was planning to be strong, and I wanted to make love to him so badly. But at the same time, I was thinking about my commitment to Kirk.

I knew I was totally in love with my chocolate boy and that this was not going to be a quick taking-care-of-my-needs type of thing. The day before we were going to meet up, I went to a local bed and breakfast and checked prices and availability. My needs and feelings got the better of me, and on the

Sunday morning of his arrival, I packed toothpaste, toothbrush, clean underwear, make-up, and whatever I needed to do my hair in my handbag, even though my smart brain was telling me, *You're not going to sleep with him.*

We had decided to meet at my business. I am sure he could hear my heart beating while he was driving up on the motorway. He arrived in style, pulling up outside my business in a Ford Probe in a sexy, unusual colour. He had a big bunch of mixed flowers and a beautiful white shirt hanging in the back of his car. He sported a ponytail with shaved back and sides. When he stepped out of his car, he was Mr GQ from head to toe. And I could smell him from afar.

As much as I tried to keep some distance between us, the energy and electricity was sparking. We went for early lunch, and the conversation flowed, and then we went for a drive afterwards. He had lots of friends in the city. As we were making our way to visit one, we changed our minds. He parked the car, and we talked about whether we were going to make love. I told him I wanted to make love to him, but I was committed to Kirk and didn't know what to do as I knew this was not going to be just a one-off need. He brought some logic to my thinking. He said, "We could do it and not like it as much as we thought we would, or we might not last. Or we don't do it and become good friends. Then when Kirk comes home, we decide to go from friends to lovers. And that would be more complicated. Or we could do it, love it, and be together forever." Then he stretched over to me and said, "Let me feel you." I surrendered. "No more questions," he said.

We drove to the bed and breakfast that I had

checked out the day before. We booked in and settled down for the night. Before we went to bed, he called his women to say goodnight. That was part of the structure of his lifestyle. My life completely changed that night. I had never had my body loved the way my chocolate boy loved my body. I had never experienced love and an orgasm at the same time. My joy of love and sex could be heard across the ocean. I was floating above the earth and happy.

During the night, I felt a presence apart from my chocolate boy. Standing by my side of the bed and looking down at me was Kirk. He was just shaking his head.

Waking up with my beautiful chocolate boy in the morning was like waking up in heaven. We made love and spent the morning together. I was floating on cloud nine, and when I walked, I was walking on clouds. If money were no object, then that was the morning we should have run away. I wanted to sing from the highest mountaintop. I had been in love before and was in love with Kirk, but nothing felt like the love I was experiencing for my chocolate boy. I did not know where it was going, but I was happy and willing to go anywhere with this love.

A few days later, Kirk called me. Right away he asked me if I had met someone as he was getting the feeling that I had. I could not hide the truth and told him I had. Not long after, he moved to a prison that was further away and more difficult for me to get to.

I could not wait to be with my chocolate boy. My girlfriend's party was back on, and he came to the city for the weekend. We had an amazing time together. A few days before Christmas, he came back down to the city, and we spent two days together. We drove back to our hometown on Christmas Eve. Sharon had arrived from Switzerland for the New Year's celebration, and the three of us saw in the new year at a nightclub, drinking champagne and dancing the night away.

It was now 1999, and by the end of January, I got my chocolate boy a job in the city, working with my friend Anne at her car rental company. He stayed with me during the week, and on weekends, he went back home. Some weekends I also went home, and we travelled back to the city together.

I will not be able to talk about the real flesh of my relationship with my chocolate boy. After nineteen years, we are still together, so I need to skirt around the fleshy part of our relationship. But what I can say is thank God my chocolate boy played the best devil's advocate in my life. He has challenged me to grow into my greatness and to become the person I am today. He showed me how to love him as he is, without loving him to change him into what I want him to be. Without his challenges in my life, I would not have stopped to analyse my life such a way that allows my greatness to grow. Relationships are not just to make ourselves feel better, but to see ourselves through the challenges that the relationship presents. We are mirrors of the dark and the light sides of each other. When we are truly in love, we are able to accept life's challenges with a deeper thinking of self. We are more willing to find solutions to the challenges that are set before us. We are open to listening, and to expressing our deepest emotions, whether they are bad or good, and sometimes even through anger. There is a fine line between love and hate; sometimes they can even become one. There are times we don't like what we see about ourselves in the mirror of those relationships made of deep love. It can make us run away and hide in deep, dark places where we feel won't be reached.

The relationship with my chocolate boy forced me to step out of myself and my comfort zone in every aspect of my physical, emotional, and spiritual existences. He has played all the unfinished lessons of every man I have loved and walked away from. And even in the darkest times of our relationship, I've never wanted to leave him. I have never questioned my love for him as I had no expectations for him to live up to. I have never told him what I wanted in a man to cause him to feel he had to be something he was not. I had already made up my mind to love him for the bad things he would do, and if I could love him after he did or said something that was hurtful or against my values, then when he did do something good, it would be a bonus.

It took some time for my chocolate boy to feel comfortable with my way of thinking and to be assured that he did not have to hide the truth from me about the way he chose to live his life. He worked at the car rental job in the city for nine months, but during that time, he had lots of pressure from the relationships he had back home, even though he was going back every weekend. In the end, he gave up the job in the city to spend more time back home. We talked on the phone about every three hours during the day.

It was now coming up to the year 2000. My family was planning a family reunion in Jamaica to celebrate our parents' fiftieth wedding anniversary. We made all the plans from England; we even baked the cakes in England. It was a busy Christmas season for me in 1999. I did not have a chance to see my chocolate boy or Sharon when she arrived from Switzerland as I had to help my sister-in-law bake the cakes, shop for a suitable wedding dress for my mother, and shop for all the other things we needed to carry down to Jamaica.

It was not the end of the world in 2000 as predicted. My parents' anniversary was on the seventeenth of January. My siblings and I were travelling to Jamaica at different times. I tried to get my chocolate boy to make the trip, but he had lots of issues with his relationships. He was still not opening up to me about these relationships, and I was not pushing him to tell me about them.

Nina, my African girlfriend, had been diagnosed with cancer. She did not want to talk to me about her full diagnosis or her life expectancy. I invited her to come with me to my family reunion in Jamaica. We travelled together to Florida and stayed for a few days before travelling to Jamaica.

When I arrived in Florida, l was expecting a phone call from Kirk. I had told him about the plans for my family celebration in Jamaica. But he did not call me.

This was a very special time for my parents. They had to walk to the church, while the cakes were carried to the reception on the heads of cake-bearers. The reception was held under a marquee made out of wood and straw, that in those days was called a *bood*. My mother had dreamed of a wedding ring with some diamonds in it, so I had taken her plain wedding band to a jeweller in Florida and had it redesigned with seven diamonds added to it, six to represent her six children and one to represent my father. We had a limousine to drive them to the church and the reception.

They both looked beautiful, and my mother was overwhelmed by the new design of her wedding ring. We had the reception at the most beautiful five-star hotel with magnificent gardens. The celebration with our family and friends was full of fun and unforgettable memories.

My parents had never slept in a hotel before, and we had to trick them to sleep in the honeymoon suite. We had packed all their church clothes without them knowing as we knew they would never miss church. Our plans were to pick them up from the hotel in the morning and take them to the church. They were not keen to sleep at the hotel, so a few of us stayed with them. That made them feel comfortable to sleep. Of course, we left when they fell asleep. In the morning, by the time my brother got to the hotel to pick them up, they had gotten a taxi to church.

The whole experience of the fiftieth anniversary will always be memorable. After the celebration, we booked three days in a beautiful hotel on the north coast of Jamaica. It was a great bonding time for me and my siblings, along with my siblings' children. And Nina joined us. We would have loved our parents to join us, but they would not leave their home. It was such a fun and joyful time we all spent together, not knowing that the clock of life was counting down for a few.

After the celebration and fun, Nina and I returned to Florida. My son had already returned to Florida as he had to go back for aviation school. We got back to Florida, and Kirk still had not called me. I was concerned, but not too much, as I was too busy to pay much attention. Besides, my thoughts were more with my chocolate boy. Nina spent all day at the mall, maxing out her credit cards. I am sure she had a feeling that her cancer was going to take her out.

Kirk eventually called me on the day I was returning to England. He was more concerned that I had spent my Christmas with Sharon and my chocolate boy. When I explained to him how busy I was with the preparation of my parents' anniversary and told him that I did not have the time to party with them, he did not want to believe me and felt that I was holding back the truth.

When I returned to England, Kirk made no attempt to communicate with me. I had prayed for God to remove one of my men from my life. Two weeks later, when I returned to Florida, I still had not heard from Kirk. In my heart, I knew I was already over him.

From the day my chocolate boy appeared in my life, I began going through a slow transition, and I knew I had to make up my mind whether I was going to live and work full-time in Florida or in England. But destiny had already taken its path in my life. My son was already in aviation school, and he needed to be more responsible in managing money and fully take control of his dreams. I had set him on the path that he had wanted since he was six years old, so it was not difficult for me to make the decision to settle permanently in England.

The universe had already started to make the changes for me. Lora, who owned the salon from which I ran my business, lost the salon's lease as they were remodelling the mall. Although many businesses approached me to work with them once they heard I was available, I did not want to work with anyone else in Florida. I was not feeling it, and it was going to take Lora time to find and set up new premises. So I settled down to a permanent life in England. It was strange not to be travelling.

My son settled into his responsibilities to become his own man, and I worked hard to pay his aviation school fees. We missed each other, but I was so proud of the way he had grown up and was taking life and his responsibilities very seriously. He moved away from Karen's house and shared an apartment with two of his friends. My son never found it difficult to study and work as he was very passionate and gifted with his choice of career.

My chocolate boy and I needed somewhere more permanent to live so we could have our own home comforts and privacy. Craig's younger brother, whom I got on with very well, was a housing officer. He worked with me to get my own apartment. I became close with my chocolate boy's family and spent some weekends with his mother, grandmother, two brothers and sister.

The millennium year went by quickly. My son came home for Christmas and New Year's. After seeing him in 2001, my chocolate boy came back to the city and lived with me for the first three months of the year. He was happy to settle in the city full-time, without the other relationships that were a big part of his life. You could say it was more an addiction for him. Just dealing with me was not enough for him, so he stayed with me for one week and then went home for one week. Now he was the one who was doing the travelling up and down. It seemed to work for us as my chocolate boy was quite a handful to have around full on while I was working.

I decided to write to Kirk as I knew it was approaching the time he was expected to be released from prison in 2002. In my letter, I asked him what date he was expected to be released. He did not reply, and I forgot about him. Then one day I unexpectedly received a letter from him, asking me how I was and if I was still with my chocolate boy. He said he did not know when he was expected to be released, but he would get in touch with me when he got home. I replied with a polite letter. I never heard from him again, and he never made contact with me once he got home. I did look him up on the internet and found a government site with all his previous details and his new address. To get his new address, all I had to do was pay twenty dollars. I was tempted, but I decided to leave it alone and not confront him. I found his son on social media, and he had posted a picture of them both. His son was all grown up and married. I sent his son a message, asking him to give his dad my regards, and he did tell him. I wanted Kirk to know that I could find him if I wanted to and give him the opportunity to show me some acknowledgement for all the support I had given him as someone I had loved. He had treated me the same way he treated the young lady who was my client who came into my facial room that day. I admit that I have looked at all his family members' profiles on social media, and none of them have him as a friend. But I know the way the universe works. He and I will meet one day, and he will have to acknowledge me and say thank you.

Nina's cancer came back, and they gave her six months to live. She went into a deep depression. She had sent her daughter to Africa as it was better for her during her illness to not have a teenager to deal with. She had made a trip to Africa and married a young man over there but was not coping well with her life expectancy and shut down. She just would not talk. I had to fight with her to write her will. I supposed doing it would make it real and final in her mind. I dealt with all the legal aspects of getting her husband over to England to be with her before she died. Two weeks before Nina died, her daughter finished high school and turned eighteen. She got back to England two days before Nina died. Nina died six months to the day the doctors had given her. It was a quiet funeral with no more than ten people.

Her daughter was now motherless and fatherless. I had to take some responsibility for this young girl. Just before Nina departed in September 2002, the landlord I was renting space from for my business died, and his wife and children were now in charge. All the time I had spent with them since I first worked in the city in 1981 counted for nothing. Things were about to turn nasty with them. Little did I know there were more clocks of life on their final countdowns. They would change the tide for me and wake a part of me that was waiting to emerge.

I was having dreams that were taking me into deep thoughts for quite some time. One of the dreams was of the deaths of my father and his brother's wife. A multitude of people turned up on the street in my hometown for my father's funeral. In the dream I got to the church late and the doors were closed. They were big, heavy doors, and I had to push hard to open them. Everyone in the church turned around and looked at me as I walked down the aisle towards the altar, where my father's coffin lay.

After the church service, I followed the crowd to a graveyard, where we buried him. His brother's wife was already in her coffin in a small kind of hut. I entered the hut, where she was lying awake in the coffin. I asked her why she was not sleeping. I awoke from the dream without getting an answer from her.

Then I had another dream, this time of my mother. There was a large crowd of people in an arena, waiting for someone to appear on the stage. And when the person they were waiting for appeared on the stage, it was my mother. I can't remember what she said to the crowd, but she was talking and crying, with blood pouring from her eyes.

Another night I dreamed of a big white wedding, again in my hometown. There was lots of cake and food and the wedding celebration was on the street. I was taking part in the wedding, but it was not I who was getting married.

It was coming to the end of 2002. I spent Christmas by myself in the city. The ringing in my ears was shorter and was ringing from one ear to the other ear. My ears were ringing and energy was building up, ready to explode. If I closed my eyes and stood still, I could feel the shift in my energy flow. The changes were going to be big, and there would not be a happy outcome.

When Christmas came to an end, my heart was very heavy. If I could have held back the doors of time leading to the new year, I would have. On New Year's Eve of 2003, I could not sleep. It was as if I was waiting for an explosion. About five o'clock, I got a call from my niece in my hometown. There had been a shooting between members of my nephew's gang; my twin nieces, their cousin, and a girlfriend were shot. I did not have time to think. I had to make all the necessary calls to my brother and sister back home to get to the hospital. My niece who had made the call had to run all the way to the house of her twin sisters and get their mother. It was sheer madness and confusion. But what was clear was that one of the twins was dead and the other was fighting for her life. The friend also died. Their cousin had injuries, but they were not serious.

By the time I switched on the television, the national morning news was already reporting it all. The news stations on the television and radio were reporting the shooting. I had always dreamed of the family name being famous, but not in this way. I went into work that morning on the bus, and some people were already talking about the incident. I wanted to shout and say, *That's my family you are talking about!*

The next day I travelled back home, and the madness started. The whole matter was taken out of the family's hands. The local government, along with community leaders, members of Parliament, and the police took over. The local and national newspapers were on us. We never had a say.

I was chosen to be the spokesperson on behalf of my brother, and I sat on the community group that was organising a large memorial service at the football ground. I was asked to give a tribute for my family. Hundreds of people from many communities turned up for the memorial tribute, and there were performances by different groups from the community. Some well-known artists also gave their support. It was televised around the world; it was a very special day.

My Tribute

We all have something in common. We are all one with God and one with all things. Therefore, we are our brothers' and sisters' keepers.

Today I would like to bring a message of peace, hope, love, and forgiveness to the world. As children of the universe, let's make a difference.

Each of us, in our own small corners of the universe, takes ownership of our brothers and sisters to make a difference in the world.

No matter what, an individual's life experience brings them to a point in their lives, and the essence of that experience, no matter at what level, is to learn to love and to forgive.

This process of love and forgiveness starts with loving and forgiving ourselves. Then we are able to love and forgive each other. Only through this process will we be able to take ownership and become our brothers' and sisters' keepers and help in nurturing and empowering each other to better govern our lives.

After the storm comes the calm, and deep in the recesses of our souls, in the stillness, there is hope for healing from all the suffering, pain, and hurt to find understanding, harmony, joy, peace, love, and forgiveness.

Peace, be still.

When it was time for the funeral, the arrangements were taken out of the family's hands as it was going to be bigger than all of us. And, of course, the families fell out as sides were drawn because my nephew and his gang were being accused of the shooting. The church chosen for the funeral service was a very small family church, and we were given twenty tickets to give to close family members. There was a television screen outside the church and on the streets. I represented my brother and my family to pay another tribute to my niece. The day went well without any trouble. I tried to get the families to work together, but there was too much anger. It was never about the shooting but about issues that were personal, ones that had nothing to do with the shooting.

A Tuesday morning, two weeks after my niece's funeral, I was sitting at my desk at work when my phone rang. With that call, my world made another 360-degree change. On the phone was one of my nieces from the United States, calling to break the news that my father had died that morning. I did not take on the shock but went into protected mood and started to make the calls to my brothers and sisters in order of the eldest to the youngest.

My sister who lived nearest Jamaica made the flight home to be with our mother. The next day, my eldest brother from the United States joined her, and a day after that, my second-eldest brother and his wife were there.

I spoke to my mother, who was inconsolable and in shock. Our mum and dad had known each other as children growing up in the same district and had been together for most of their lives. Our dad's funeral was a big affair, not with just family but also with people from communities in England, in town, and from the mountaintop we were all born on.

My chocolate boy was by my side, along with my son. We had two church services, one for the community in the town and the other on our mountaintop. Our father had been the pastor at churches in the town and on our mountaintop. He pastored many funerals, and now it was his turn to be pastored.

We all rallied around our mum, and she held it together. The first service in town started at ten in the morning. The church was filled to capacity inside, the crowd overflowing the building. Our mother requested that all her children and grandchildren sing "Great Is Thy Faithfulness" in honour of our father's faithfulness to her, his children, and his community. We made it through the song without any tears. Then I read his eulogy.

By early afternoon, with a police escort, we made our way up to our mountaintop, to the church our father had helped build as a young carpenter. The church also doubled as a school. Looking down from the plateau where the church was situated, one could see our house, the first land my father had bought at fifteen and where he had built his first home, where all his children were born.

By the time we arrived on the mountaintop, our family was waiting, a lifetime of family whom our father had taken care of. It was a glorious day on the mountaintop. The blue sky was so close, I could reach up and touch it. It was hot with a sweet, cool breeze. Father was laid to rest in the front yard of our home, looking over at the beautiful mountain. We have many big trees in our yard. The closest to our father's grave is a big eucalyptus tree. While we were singing and laying our father to rest, a great wind blew the eucalyptus tree, and big raindrops fell on a few people, including me and my chocolate boy.

The period of our father's transition and the preparation for his going-home celebration was the best time of my life. All my family was together in the country where I was born, celebrating our father's life with great passion. My chocolate boy was able to meet up with his father, whom he had not seen for years. If I could have my father back just for him to die again so I could relive the whole celebration of his life, it would be perfect.

Our father's death was going to be the biggest adjustment for our mother. Not having anyone to look after was going to be a challenge for her as she had been a carer for most of her life. We divided the house, creating a self-contained unit that we rented to a young couple. The wife turned out to be our mother's cousin. Mom occupied the larger portion of the house.

I promised to call her at the same time every day so she would have something to look forward to. It was helpful to call her at the same time every day as her hearing was not good. My siblings had their special days when they called her, and we all took turns to visit her.

A few months later, the family was blessed with good news. My son and his wife were going to have a baby.

I got involved with different community projects in my hometown. I had my own idea of a community engagement project I wanted to develop and wanted

to learn more about how they worked. None of
the current community engagement projects were
working. From what I observed, the people who
ran them fought against and sabotaged each other's
programmes.

The youths created their own laws. My nephew was
arrested for the New Year's shooting of my nieces,
their cousin, and their girlfriend. Our family was
now well and truly divided, and nothing of substance
came out of the shooting to heal and rebuild the
community. There were so many secrets between the
community and the leaders. It was not just that they
could not get themselves together; it was that they did
not *want* to get themselves together to make changes.

I decided to pursue my idea of setting up a
community engagement project. I got my proposal
together and took it to the Home Office. I was passed
from one organisation to the other with no joy. I later
found out that my idea was rolled out right across the
country. All the community organisations' concepts
were good, but they did not deliver the service. It
was also difficult for me to find motivated people to
commit to my ideas.

The aim of my idea was to support parents and their
children in finding common ground to grow together.
I did find four people to work with me during the
process. I found that it is always the community
politics and people's own personal issues that kill
ideas. We did manage to secure some funding and ran
a six-week workshop for young mothers with their
children.

During the experience of running the workshop,
I felt that it would be better for me to equip myself
with diverse skills so I could deliver the workshops

myself. The journey led me to take two courses as a facilitator in parenting and sexual health. I was always interested in homelessness and drug and alcohol addiction.

The case against my nephew and the gang-related shooting of my niece and the friend led to a conviction. He was sentenced to twenty-three years. He was twenty-three years old at the time.

It was now October 2004, and my beautiful granddaughter was born. My chocolate boy and I travelled to Florida a week after she was born. What a happy time that was for me!

We also travelled to Jamaica. This was my first visit home to Jamaica since my father had died. It was then I felt the emptiness of the months since my father's death. I did not really mourn his death as I had some wonderful journeys and a better relationship with him at night through my dreams. He spent quality time with me and showed me the kind of love I'd always wanted from him as a child and a young girl. He showed me in my dreams that he was fond of my chocolate boy.

Whenever my siblings and I went home to visit our parents, Father was always at the front gate, looking out for us. As soon as he saw us, he would shout out to our mother, who was always in the kitchen doing the finishing touches to her delicious cooking. Mum would come running out of the kitchen to join Dad at the front gate to greet us. But on this visit, it was just the memory of our father at the front gate, and the hole in my heart opened like it had the day he walked into the big bird. My mother was a broken woman. She had lost her joy for life, and the front gate was now empty.

My mother threw away her rule book and allowed me and my chocolate boy to sleep together in her house without being married.

When we arrived back to England, my work environment was about to change. After the death of the owner of the property where I ran my business, his wife and children were in charge of the premises. I met the wife on the street one day, and she gave me two weeks' verbal notice to vacate the premises. I kind of knew that it was going to happen at some point, and I had been looking for new premises, but nothing was coming up.

Then my girlfriend Nadine, whom I had known for fifteen years, approached me regarding working together. She was looking for a hairdressing salon and offered me space to rent for my beauty clinic. It was a good opportunity for me and a chance to increase my business. So with my own needs at stake, I helped her to find a great location. While I was waiting for Nadine's premises to be completed, I had given my two weeks' notice at my current location. The wife and children of the late owner were getting nasty with me. They were converting the premises into self-contained bedsit accommodations. As I was occupying the first floor, they had started the work from the top floor. By the time they had finished the top floor, I was still not in a position to move, and they started to abuse me. Bear in mind I had known the wife and her husband before their children were born and had helped to grow their business. She cut off my water supply and toilet, and threatened to bury me in the premises. I had to take out a court order for her to stop the building work, and this upset her even more. By January 2005, we settled out of court. I used the law firm of Nadine's boyfriend, and they cheated me out of money.

By then I was totally drained of all my energy, and the new premises were not ready. So, I decided to work from home, which I did for a month or two. Then Nadine finally became the leaseholder of the new premises, and we had to find building contractors and salon suppliers. I did all the footwork, and she made all the mistakes. She asked me for my experience, but when I gave it to her, she did not use anything I suggested or recommended. I soon realised she was just a chancer, dreaming the wrong dream, and had no personality for running a service business. She was one of those people who had observed someone with the gift of running a service business and making a good income because they love what they do. She thought it looked easy and believed if she did the same, she could also make a good income. She was like a thief, stealing something she did not know how to work.

From the start, the whole thing was a disaster. She allowed her family members, whom she had not had a relationship with for ten years, to come on board with their advice. She allowed her brother, who was suitable for nothing more than being ignorant, to advise her. Nadine thrived on causing conflict; where there was none, she wound up her brother to defend her. Neither of them had the capacity to run a service business. They made my life hell and almost killed me. Their destructive energy ruined my health and my business during this period.

However this experience forced me to grow into another level of my greatness mentally, emotionally, and spiritually. I worked on my self-awareness and my self-development in every aspect of my personal growth. My new location was a busy shopping area in the community where I lived.

I befriended Warren, a young white man who was a drug addict and lived on the street. I got to know him well and looked out for him every day, giving him food and clothes. He told me how he had come to live on the street. He was born in a small town in the countryside. His father left him and his mother and not having much to do in a small country town, he said it was easy when a drug dealer turned up offering him a good time. Warren became an addict, but he managed to clean himself up and decided to come to the city to be with his father. He lived with his father but got back into drugs, but this time, he was selling them instead.

He met a beautiful mixed-race girl and fell in love with her. They moved in together, and he gave her everything. He was doing well dealing drugs, but his girlfriend left him, and he fell apart. Warren started using his own drugs, and before he knew it, he had lost everything and was begging on the street. He gave up drugs but became an alcoholic, which can be harder to give up than street drugs. I tried to encourage him to take up the support of the local street drug workers.

Warren was a tall and handsome young man, but some mornings when I turned up for work, he would be lying in the road where he had fallen from being so drunk. He'd be all messed up as he would have urinated and defecated on himself. This caused a traffic jam as the cars waited for the ambulance to come and take him to hospital.

By afternoon, he would be back on the streets in

hospital scrubs in the freezing cold.

It was January 2006. I returned to work after the Christmas and New Year's break. After a few days, I wondered what had happened to Warren as I had not seen him since I had returned. So I started asking around, talking with the other homeless people. Then I bumped into one person I knew he hung around with, and he told me that Warren had died. A group of boys had kicked his head in as he lay on the sidewalk drunk. This was greatly upsetting to me.

My Youth Parents Partnership for Progress community programme was not getting support from some of the members, and I felt I could learn a lot more from volunteering with other established community programmes in the city. Not long after considering volunteering for another project, I was reading the local newspaper and came across an advert for black and minority ethnicity (BME) training to become a drug and alcohol worker. This was just what I had been looking for. I wrote my letter of application, was interviewed, and was accepted for the training programme. It was onward and upward.

I met some very interesting people from all walks of life in the course of the training. After our training, we were interviewed by various community projects about drug and alcohol users and homelessness. We were to choose where we would best fit. My first volunteer position was with a mentoring project call Red Kite. They worked with all the community projects that supported drug and alcohol users and homeless people, meeting them at the jail, escorting them to court, finding them short- and long-term accommodations —including beds for the night— and pointing them in the direction of where to get

hot food, clothes, and furniture. They also helped
them apply for their birth certificates and benefits.
Volunteers escorted them to hospital, helped them
deal with the needle exchange programme and
helped clients in their short-term intervention
rehabilitation homes, sitting with them during their
counselling programme. I also ran some of my
own projects, such as make-up and meditation. All
the drug services came under the umbrella of the
Hackney Drugs and Alcohol Team (HDAT).

As I was a volunteer, they paid for some very
expensive courses for me. I had already paid for
parenting and sexual health courses, and I wanted to
learn more. I chose a course that would also help me
deal with my own emotions, learning the emotional
freedom technique (EFT), or tapping technique,
which is used in private practice instead of cognitive
behaviour therapy (CBT).

It was during this training that I started to look at
my emotional behaviour from childhood to adulthood
and the choices I had made. The funny thing is that
the three days of training were in Leeds, where I had
had my heart operation. It was not the first time I
had gone back to Leeds since my heart operation.
Some years earlier, I had been invited to appear on a
cable television programme with some other skincare
professionals.

On this visit, I was staying in a small village. There
were about fifteen professionals on the course, and I
was the only black person. I could not sleep the night
after the first day of the course; there was a conveyor
belt running across my mind with memories from
childhood. One of the memories that came up was of
my mother and me on our way home from a hospital

appointment in town; we had missed the truck
that would take us to our mountaintop. In Jamaica,
nightfall comes quickly, without any warning, and the
darkness is dark.

We had to walk home, and If we were to take the
long road, we would never make it before nightfall.
However the shortcut home meant we would have to
cross a river. My mother decided to take the shortcut.
When we got to the river, it was not running fast, but
that can change in the blink of an eye. You have to
cross at the right point and step on the right stones.
My mother put me on her back, pulled up her skirt
around me to secure me on her back, and skilfully
picked her way across the river on just the right
stones. That was just one of the powerful memories
that came up that night. It showed me how much my
mother and father loved me. Although there were no
words, their actions spoke volumes of their love, and
they did their best.

Not only was there a convoy of memories that night,
but also I sat on the toilet most of the night with vile-
smelling diarrhoea.

For the next three days, there were plenty of
tears. I used the EFT to work through my life of old
memories and beliefs that were not my own, as well
as newer issues. This was the start of really healing
my soul.

One morning I had a present-moment dream
about Craig. I dreamed that my mother, my
younger brother, and I were walking down a dirt
road somewhere in Africa. It was not a place that I
recognised. As we walked down the road, we came
to a house with a high gate. A few black men were
sitting outside the gate. Somehow, I knew it was

Craig's house. We stopped and asked them if he was in. They opened the gate and let us in. Someone at the reception desk directed us to take the lift to the next floor, saying he would be in room number two. We followed the instructions and found room number two. My brother decided he was going to wait outside. My mother and I went into the room, and Craig was lying on a bed. Next to the bed was a couch, like that of a dentist. We sat on the bed with him. He started showing my mother photographs of me when I lived in Florida. They were photographs that I had sent him for real when I lived in Florida that he had asked me to send. He told my mother how much he cared for me and said that he wished he had treated me better. He had tears in his eyes.

I awoke from the dream, and I knew it was real. I picked up my phone and called Craig's number. I expected it to be ringing in Africa, but it rang in England. Craig did not wait for me to say hello. He just said, "Norma, I am sick." I asked him where he was, and he gave the phone to a nurse, who gave me details of where he was. I had never gotten ready so fast. In three hours, I was walking down the road I had just dreamed about. When I got to the gate, I went to reception and was told to take the lift to the first floor, to room number two. Everything was like in my dream. When I entered the room, Craig was lying on a bed, and next to the bed was a couch, like the one in my dream. Nursing assistants were just lifting him out of the bed and strapping him on to the couch.

Craig was in the final stage of multiple sclerosis. The nursing assistants left the room, and he started to cry. He could not believe I could still care for him with all the mean things he had done and said to me. He was sad that we had known each other for twenty years and did not have a child as evidence that we had had a relationship. Little did he know that if my plans had worked out, things would have been different, and we would have had a child. I wiped the tears from his eyes. He believed that he was sick because of voodoo performed by the girl whom he was living with in Africa. They had a son, and she was upset that he never married her, so she left him with their son. Craig did not know where she was, and from the moment she left, he got really sick. He talked about some of the things he had done to me and said how sorry he was. He told me he realised I was the best woman for him and wondered if he asked, would come back to Africa with him? Of course, I said that I would.

He never asked me if I was in a relationship with anyone. He pretended I was still waiting for him, and I never told him anything different. Craig wanted to keep it that way as he realised what he had with me. I stayed with him till he got tired of talking, and every day, I sent him text messages and called him once or twice a week. I told him I loved him as in a little corner of my heart, I had kept a place for him over the years.

I had never forgotten his birthday, so on the Monday morning of his birthday, I called him. His phone rang in Africa. He answered and sounded strong, and I knew he was ready to die. He was so surprised that I remembered his birthday. He had just arrived in Africa from England. Craig asked me if he were to send me a ticket if I would come to Africa to be with him, and I again said yes. He said he would give his brother, who had accompanied him back to Africa, the ticket as he was returning to England on Saturday. Craig knew, and I knew fully well, that that was not going to happen as there was no more time left for him, and I would never have left my chocolate boy. But it was a way for him to say that he was sorry and that he did care for me, and I wanted him to know that there was a place in my heart for him.

After that Monday, he fell into a coma. He died on the Thursday. He came to say goodbye and lay beside me in my dreams. Craig visited me quite a few times, one time with us in Africa. The last time he visited me, he was with me and my mother in Jamaica, in the house where I was born. He asked my mother if he could marry me. She said yes, and he gave me a ring. I cleaned out a drawer for him to put his clothes in. We found peace, and he has not visited me again.

My relationship with my chocolate boy was teaching me so much about myself. The relationship was very challenging, but it taught me the real art of forgiveness, along with other challenges around my business with Nadine. She was not the girl I knew before we had gone into business together. She was envious and clueless. She had no idea how to run a business and no talent as a hairdresser. She wanted everything for herself and blamed me in every way. Nadine just made life uncomfortable for me.

In 2008, Sharon married her second husband, and my chocolate boy and I went to Switzerland for her wedding. It was one of those magical times for us. We had three amazing days and one night of dancing. We were young and beautiful, enjoying a touch of the good life and sweet love.

Life was going by quickly, and I felt stuck in my

relationship with my chocolate boy. Things were not turning out the way I had dreamed they would. And even though we had plenty of quality time together, I became conscious that my life was all about him and his life. I felt lost. Thank God my volunteer work kept me grounded.

My fiftieth birthday came out of nowhere, and I decided to spend the day by myself. I know it may sound crazy, but I spent the day writing my eulogy. I wrote down all the instructions I wanted to be followed in the event of my death. I did a lot of reflection on that day, and I felt as if I did not know where my life was going.

Finally, I did get something out of the day. I always had wanted to practise meditation. I did some research online and found a wonderful meditation centre to go to. I grew spiritually and found online a multitude of mentors who resonate my truth. I got strong in order to deal with Nadine. I ran weekly meditation classes for my clients. As I got deeper into my self-healing and my deeper self, I had the opportunity to go on a pirate radio station one morning and do a live meditation. I was very surprised by the number of people who called in, including a lot of men. One young lady called me to say I had saved her life as she was just in the act of taking her life. I spent some time to support her.

As I grew spiritually, I wanted to go deeper into my own self-healing. I came across a course in chakra psychology. Again, the people running the course were all professionals. This course took you back to when you were in your mother's womb, and from birth, you were to think deeply and completely from childhood, focusing on the energy that runs through your body and deals with all your emotions.

The group was safe and supportive about the second chakra, which deals with emotions, desires, and pleasures. Some of the students were talking about their experiences of being raped and sexually abused. The ones who were professional counsellors shared their clients' experiences. I could not understand why they allowed the experiences to destroy their lives and cause them to have difficulties enjoying intimacy.

When I think or talk about my sexual experiences, I see that it was my comfort and my power that helped me to survive my childhood of feeling unloved and abandoned.

When we got to the heart chakra, I was on the floor crying uncontrollably, where I stayed for most of the class. I felt all the emotions that I had been carrying in my heart from the day my two grandmothers died and my dad left on the big bird.

A few days after the class, I called my eldest brother to ask him how long after my father had left that both my grandmothers died and I became ill with my heart. He told me that it all happened within three months. I then called my doctor to arrange to see my medical notes as I lacked information regarding my illness and my operation. I wondered if my parents knew or understood what the real problem was with my heart, and if the doctors had properly and clearly informed them. They just knew I had a hole in my heart and that the doctors were going to fix it. My dad was asked to choose between a pig valve or a plastic valve to replace my heart valve. So reading my medical notes gave me the full information of what the problem was with my heart. I was then able to do my research and understand the mitral valve, what it does, and where in the heart it is.

One rainy Sunday morning, I made my way to the house where I had lived with the lady and her husband when I first arrived in England. Everything looked smaller. It was an address that I had passed many times over the years without realising that it was where I once had lived. Not only was the house still there, but so was the doctor's surgery where she had registered me.

I rang the bell of the surgery, and an old lady came to the door. I explained to her my story, and she invited me in. She had kept the surgery area just the same as it was all those years ago. She told me she was the nurse who had helped her husband with the surgery, adding that I would have had contact with her. She told me that the people who had owned the house I lived in, sold it. The downstairs was a self-contained flat, and the upstairs was rented out by the room. She encouraged me to ring the bell as the tenants were nice people; she felt sure they would let me in. I kept her company for a while and talked about the past.

I went next door. Before I rang the bell, I stood at the door to feel the energy of my father. I wanted to get a sense of how he must have felt waiting with his hat in his hands, not knowing how I would react to him. I rang the doorbell. The couple who lived downstairs were home. The lady answered the door, and I told her my story. She called her husband and they invited me in, showed me around, and allowed me some time to feel the space and energy. The tenants who had the room that I had stayed in were also in and they invited me into the room, but I was happy just to stand and look. Everything seemed smaller. I started to get emotional and left. I stood outside in the rain, looking at the house. I cried as all the memories and pain mixed with my tears.

It was at that moment I realised how much my father had loved me and what sacrifice he had made to give me and all his children his best. He was silent but faithful to the end. Having all the pieces of information, I was able to appreciate my father's challenges, his strength, his devotion, and his love, not just for me, but also for the family he had created. The burdens that I had carried as a five-year-old child seeing my father going into the belly of the big bird, and flying away fell out of my body and were replaced by peace.

I continued to do more volunteer work and achieved more qualifications. My business was not performing the way it should have been with all the clients I had attracted over the years. The working environment with Nadine was getting more toxic. I knew she was spreading rumours, saying that I was envious of her. The atmosphere she created in the shop could have exploded and killed both of us. I tried to find new premises, but no doors opened for me to get away from this soul-destroying situation. Although I was strong, every so often, I could feel my heart beating off its rhythm. Some weeks I hardly made enough money, only enough to pay Nadine the rent. I was not getting any benefits from working.

The only thing that was keeping me alive was doing my meditation. I meditated several times a day, and it really supported me and carried me through all the business drama.

My relationship with my chocolate boy became

more comforting as the years rolled by. But for our mother, no matter how many visitors she had, including my siblings and me, it was not what she wanted. I kept my promise to her; no matter where I was at eight o'clock every day, I called her. She was just not happy. She was so used to getting what she wanted, and what she wanted was for me to be with her. It was not possible for me to do that, so she was not happy. What we did not want was for her to lose her independence and give up.

Her hearing was getting worse. She did all the talking. She was mobile and more than capable of doing everything for herself, but she wanted one of her children with her for comfort. The loneliness without our father was getting to her. She developed shingles, which was very painful for her. My older brothers took turns spending a long period of time with her. Every Tuesday morning, she would get very sad and relive the moment our father died.

I visited her by myself and then stopped off in Florida to spend time with my son and granddaughter. My younger sister also spent a good amount of time with our mother, and so did my older sister. My younger sister and I were very concerned as our mum was approaching eighty-two, the age our father was due to turn just before he died.

At the beginning of 2012, I knew it was going to be a life-changing year. One night in June 2012, Dad came to visit me in a dream. He stood on the left side at the end of my bed. Dressed in the suit he had been buried in, I asked him if it was time for her to go. He said yes, it was, but every time I remembered the dream to tell my sister or any of my siblings, I would lose the consciousness of the thought. It was as if something did not want me to interfere with my mother's journey and the way she was supposed to die.

Then three weeks before her eighty-second birthday, on a Thursday, I called her as usual. There was a family friend with her. Mum was crying; she felt like her head was exploding. I talked with the family friend. She said I should not worry, adding that she would make sure to take care of my mother. I went to call my sister, but something interrupted me, and I forgot.

That night we had a call from my mother's niece; Mom was in hospital. My younger sister made up her mind to take some sabbatical time from work and go and look after our mother. Even then I did not remember to tell her that our dad had paid me a visit and said it was time for Mom to go.

By Sunday, it looked as if my mother was recovering. All my siblings had managed to talk to her, and she had plenty of visitors. My cousins remained with her around the clock. Then on Monday, my mother told the doctors that she was ready to die. She thanked them for their care and prayed for them. She prayed for a cleaner and the other patients. Mom told my cousin to call the undertaker she had used to look after our father. My cousin did not want to do that. My mother told my cousin that she was going on a journey, adding that my cousin could only go halfway with her. Mom would tell her when she needed to let her go on alone, but she was not to worry as my dad was there with her, looking handsome and happy.

Mom went to sleep, but when she woke up on Tuesday morning, she told my cousin it was time for her to go on alone. She asked my cousin to tell all her children that she loved us very much and that we must live good, not just with each other, but also with our cousins and the larger family. My mother, telling my cousin she must go now, took her last breath, three hours before my father had taken his.

On Monday night, I could not sleep. I got out of bed and sat on the sofa, holding the energetic space with my mother. She allowed me to travel with her on her journey at about three in the morning. My chocolate boy woke up and asked me why I was not coming to bed. I told him my mother was dying, saying I had to stay with her till she made her transition. By six-thirty, she had parted company with me and took her last human breath. My sister called me just before 7 a.m., and before she told me, I told her Mum was gone. It was then I told her that our father had visited with me and told me it was time for her to go.

The preparation for our mother's homegoing was so much easier as we already had a template from our father's homegoing. Our mother's death brought different emotional challenges for each of us. None of us had any idea what emotional feelings were lying deep within us that would slowly creep up on all of us.

It was comforting to know that my mother had prepared herself to go home and had no fear. One of her greetings every day when I called her was "I'm still in the land of the living." Both our parents had a strong belief in God.

Our mother's homegoing service was the same as our father's. But by the time we got to our mountaintop, the heavens opened, and it began to rain. It would not stop raining. We had to wait it out in the church. The rain stopped very late in the afternoon, with just enough time before it turned dark to lay our mother to rest.

When we came down from our mountaintop, we heard the news that the rain was turning into a hurricane. I was due to travel to Florida the next day to spend two days with my son and granddaughter, but all flights had been cancelled.

I stayed another day with my siblings. With our mother gone, this was going to be a big adjustment for all of us. This was a challenge that bought out all kinds of issues for all of us. We retreated into our personal spaces. It took two years before we could deal with those challenges.

My mother spent nine months with me after her going home. She always visited with my father and he stood behind her shoulder but never spoke to me. My mother never spoke to me with her voice; it was always done telepathically. During the months of her visits, I felt she was a little upset that she had died without any of her children at her side.

My chocolate boy was a great source of comfort, love, and strength. But soon it was my chocolate boy's turn to experience his share of grief and pain. He lost his half-brother in a car accident on New Year's Eve of 2013. His father came to England from Jamaica for the funeral, and we all spent good quality time with him after the funeral, before he returned to Jamaica. Then, twelve months later, my chocolate boy's father was shot and killed in his house in Jamaica. I was not able to go with my chocolate boy to Jamaica, but by then, my second-eldest brother and his wife had moved back to Jamaica and were there to give my chocolate boy and his brother support on my behalf. About six months later, my chocolate boy's grandmother died, and the day after, they found his sister dead in her bed.

Life was changing fast. I lived through this period of my life on meditation. To find my new path, I made energetic contact with some very powerful spiritual mentors. All I wanted was to keep growing into my greatness. My life was changing, and the business relationship was truly over with Nadine. If I had not gotten to the point of my greatness through meditation and using the energy of love, she would have totally destroyed me. I would not have been able to come back from the physical challenges that had taken a toll on my health without my knowledge. The time was right for me to find somewhere else to work.

The new business address was no better than working at Nadine's place in terms of personality. The owner was a male version of Nadine. The only thing that made him different was that he was Turkish.

But the universe had a plan for me. I was uncomfortable in this new space. I shared the space with the other people who worked for the shop. They had first choice about working in the space. The love and support of all my clients kept me strong, and they showed up to use my services.

As I watch the children play from my kitchen window, I see the memories that they are making.

I hear the laughter they are laughing.

This window I am looking through

Is not the window of my dreams.

It's not the window I had dreamed to be looking through.

Yet those children playing have no other thoughts,

Only happy times that will stay with them forever and bring smiles to their faces.

But my memory is saying this is not the picture of my dreams.

In 2014, my physical body could not take any more. I knew I was reliving age five. I could hear my heart beating off rhythm, and my digestive system started acting up. I knew I had to go to the hospital, but I was trying to put things in place as I did not know how bad things were going to be or whether they would have to operate on me immediately. On the day I checked into a hospital, as soon as the nurse took my blood pressure, she got me a wheelchair and took me straight into the emergency department. They kept me in hospital for two weeks and got my heart rhythm under control. I was not happy with the hospital or the consultant. As soon as I left the hospital, I asked my doctor to make an appointment at the hospital of my choice, along with an appointment with a consultant. I had to draw on all my knowledge and strength from doing the journey before and the new strengths and knowledge that I now had. I was more satisfied with the new choice of hospital and consultant recommended to me by my girlfriend Angel. I had known her for ten years. Over the years, we had developed a strong friendship. She also had a mitral heart valve condition. She was afraid of having her replacement operation, even after I shared my experience that I was the only survivor of the first mitral valve replacement performed in England. We started going to hospital appointments together to see the heart consultant. I asked the consultant to add me to Angel's surgeon's operating list.

I arranged to work from home as it was much better for me and it reduced the running around between appointments.

When my new consultant had a closer look at my heart, he found that my tricuspid valve on the right side was also in trouble and needed to be repaired with atrial fibrillation. So my heart was in far more trouble this time around.

Working from home allowed me to have more time to write, and after my operation, I would be able to work during my recovery. In working from home, I found peace and was able to take better care of myself physically and spiritually. As I prepared myself for my operation, I changed my diet, detoxed my body, meditated to heal my mind and body, and watched videos on mitral valve and tricuspid valve repair operations. I researched the different kinds of valves that were available through the NHS, and the pros and cons and side effects of blood thinners, including Warfarin. I also researched what I should and shouldn't eat while taking Warfarin.

During my preparation for having open-heart surgery, I had many appointments with my consultant at the hospital to do the necessary tests and evaluations. I received a letter from the hospital setting up an appointment. Having thought it was just for another procedure, I did not read the letter. I just put the date and time into my diary.

Angel had spoken to her surgeon about me, and I was looking forward to meeting her surgeon, as I had requested for him to do my operation. On the day of my appointment, I had to wait a long time to be seen as the clinic was running late. When I was eventually called in for my appointment by a nurse, a doctor in scrubs was sitting quietly in the room. The nurse introduced him to me as "Professor". After saying hello, I asked, "Why am I seeing you?"

"I'm the doctor who's going to fix your heart."

I looked at him in a funny way and said, "I didn't ask for you."

He said, "You can have whichever doctor you want to do your operation. Which doctor did you ask for?"

In that moment, I could not remember the name of the surgeon I had asked for, so I asked if I could call my friend to get his name. I tried to call Angel, but could not get a signal. So I said to this doctor, "I need to see whether my heart wants you to rummage around with it."

"How are you going to know this?"

"Go along with me for a minute." He agreed, so I held up my right hand and asked him to put his right hand in my right hand. "Let's sit in silence for a few moments." So he placed his right hand in mine, and for that moment, our hearts felt each other's hearts. I knew right away that he was the right surgeon for me; my heart had chosen him. "Yes, let's do it," I told him.

We talked about the operation as the procedures were not the same as when I was a child. I was happy to have a cow tissue valve, which would last me for fifteen years, and I would only have to take blood thinners for the first three months. But if there were any complications during the operation, the doctor would have to make the best choice for me. He and his nurse looked at his diary and gave me a choice between the first week in March or the last week in April 2017.

After my appointment with Professor, and to prepare myself for surgery, I did my research on him and read some of his publications. I gave his details to my younger sister, and she did her research on him with the help of a high-profile doctor whom she looks after. She found that the two of them had been best friends for ten years and their families spent time together. This high-profile doctor had told my sister that Professor had done all the heart operations for his family. I could not have gotten a better surgeon to do my surgery.

In the months that followed, I made all my aftercare preparations with my younger sister, my chocolate boy, and my close friends. I made plans for them to take turns in supporting me. I was expected to be in hospital for six days after my surgery, and the majority of my recovery would be at home. I prepared myself physically, financially, and with my clients, and, most of all, with my spiritual and mental selves. I meditated on the best outcome for my recovery. I had watched so many videos of mitral heart valve replacement and tricuspid valve repairs that if I were able to open my own chest, I could have performed my own operation.

I also researched different people's recoveries. I was expected to take Warfarin for three months. It was a medication that I strongly objected to taking when I had first become ill. I could not understand why I had to take it as when I was a child, I did not take blood-thinning medication. I only took medication when I had to stay in hospital, and after my first heart surgery, I never took any medication, not even aspirin, for fifty-two years. I was not very happy with taking Warfarin. This was going to be my biggest issue. There were other options for blood thinners, but I was told Warfarin was the best one as it required regular checks to make sure my blood was not clotting.

The next appointment I had was with Professor's practice nurse to do all the last-minute checks and to prepare me for the process ahead. She told me the date I was scheduled for my operation. It was three weeks past my expected date and three days before my sixty-second birthday. This would be a rebirth for me.

> *Memories are there to remind us*
> *where we are coming from, where we*
> *are going,*
> *and where we don't want to be.*

Life is perfect. Everything we do is perfect. Nothing in life happens by chance, even the things that we think are bad. It's up to us to find our own divine purposes amid the mysteries of life. I believe no one is wrong and no one is right. It's just the experience that is right for each of us. As we move forward, life comes to us. Even if we live in a dark cupboard, we will meet life. The consciousness of thinking will bring it to us, as nothing can stop the force of the universe. Our greatest good is always calling us, as whatever we resist persists.

When I was a child, I was an observer of my life as I had no control or choice. Now I am a participant, participating in my life, as I now have control and the experience to be part of the best outcome of my well-being.

On 19 March 2017, I checked into a beautiful, brand-new five-star hospital in the city. My younger sister, my chocolate boy, my niece, and Anne accompanied me to check in for my open-heart surgery scheduled for Monday morning, 20th March 2017. When we got to the cardiothoracic ward to check in, they had no beds as most of the patients who were due to be discharged had to stay longer. So we waited for them to find me a bed on another ward. They found a bed for me on the sixth floor. There was just me, another lady who had had her surgery and was waiting to go home, and a lovely old black lady in the side room. She was due to have the new style of valve replacement, where they go up through the groin, collapse the old valve, and open up the new one. She was in her eighties and could not have open-heart surgery.

It was hard to let my loved ones go, and I knew this

was hard for them too. My sister and my chocolate boy would be back at seven in the morning to see me to the operating theatre and to wait until the operation was over.

The lady who was waiting to be discharged that evening had a mechanical heart valve replacement. We had a good talk before she left. Then I was left on my own with only the old lady in the side room.

A doctor came to see me to explain how the operation would go, adding that if there was anything that I did not understand, he would be happy to talk it through with me. My main concern was being addicted to morphine, but he assured me that by taking the medicine only to relieve pain, I would not get addicted as addiction to morphine only happens when the medicine is taken without pain.

I found it difficult to switch off in order to sleep, as this was real. In a few hours, I would be on my second journey of open-heart surgery. I made two videos that I wanted to post on Facebook as I did not tell many people I was having open-heart surgery, but the internet connection at the hospital was not good. I was not able to upload my videos, so I meditated and visualised, and eventually fell asleep.

I was up at five, and I called my chocolate boy to wake him up as I had booked a cab to pick him up at six o'clock. He said he was getting up, but at six, I had a call from the cab company to say they were outside the apartment and were calling my chocolate boy, but he was not answering. So I called him, and he told me he didn't think he could make it as he had diarrhoea, but he would come to the hospital in the afternoon. I almost lost my joy as I wanted things to be different this time, with my chocolate boy standing in for my father, and my younger sister standing in for my mother. My chocolate boy had feared not diarrhoea; he feared he could not handle seeing me going to the theatre, knowing what was going to happen to me. I had to quickly adjust my feelings as it was not the time to allow myself to feel let down or lose my momentum to create my best outcome. I held onto my mantra, "I'm a peaceful soul."

The second journey of my heart surgery was different for me as I was conscious and had a better understanding of life and more maturity. And this time I had all the information and had made the choice myself.

My younger sister arrived at seven and helped me to take a shower as I had to wash properly with some special antiseptic body wash. My sister took charge of my phone and all my personal belongings. At a quarter to eight, a porter who looked just like my dad in every way arrived with a wheelchair to take me to the operating theatre.

So the three of us made the journey to the theatre. Our energy was peaceful as we arrived at the long corridor, looking down at all the operating theatres. There was no turning back. When we reached the point where my sister was not allowed to go any further, we said, "See you later." The porter pushed me and my wheelchair down the long corridor to the operating theatre I would be in. I looked back to see my sister standing there. As I waved to her, it was like looking down a tunnel. All the love I had for her filled my heart. I felt good knowing that her heart would be beating for me as mine was been repaired.

In the anaesthetic room was a trainee and the anaesthetist. The connection between me and the anaesthetist was instant. I told him the story of when I first met Professor. I asked him to tell Professor that we were also connected through my sister and his good family friend. He told me he also knew this friend. I also told him about the book I was writing as we were chatting and laughing.

The next thing I knew, I saw my mother standing on my right, wearing a pink dress with a matching pink hat. She never said a word to me; she just watched. Then the next thing I remember was waking up to my sister's voice, but all I wanted to do was to sleep.

On Tuesday, the day after my surgery, I had to wake up to have some soup. My sister tried to feed me the soup, but I was happy to keep sleeping. Then my chocolate boy took over and got me to drink all the soup. I drifted in and out of sleep but felt so much comfort from the energy of my chocolate boy and my sister. My chocolate boy returned home on Tuesday evening and kept in touch with my sister and the hospital until I was able to speak with him on the phone.

On Tuesday night, my heart stopped beating many times because of my atrial fibrillation. But on Wednesday morning, I woke up fully and was making good progress. Thursday, the twenty-third of March, I awoke to my sixty-second birthday. I was more conscious of my surroundings and of the fact that I had just survived open-heart surgery. The nurses and doctors came and sang "Happy Birthday" to me. When my sister came, she brought cakes for the staff. A few of my close friends came to visit and were allowed in one by one.

On Thursday morning I was due to leave intensive care and move to a high-dependency ward. The night sister came to see me before she went off duty. She wanted to ask me a question before I moved from intensive care. She said that on Monday night, she had an emergency and had to call Professor, who was still operating, to come to the ward to see a patient who was having a crisis. After he had attended to the patient, he asked her where his soulmate was. She asked him whom he was referring to, and he told her to never mind, he would find his soulmate. The night nurse said he found my bed and checked to make sure I was doing OK. So she wanted to know why he had called me his soulmate. I said I could not tell her why, but she said I had to tell her as Tuesday night she had had to work on my heart as it had stopped many times, and that made her my soulmate too. So I told her the story of when I first met Professor and how I had gotten him to connect with my heart. And then I found out that my sister had taken care of his close family friend. I thanked the night sister for looking after me, and we agreed we were truly soulmates.

By lunchtime, I was moved to the high-dependency ward, and one of the registrar doctors came by to see me. He told me that they had not been able to replace my valve with a cow tissue replacement as they could not find one in the right size, so I had to have a mechanical valve placed, which meant I had to take Warfarin for the rest of my life. I had to quickly get over my disappointment. l was not going to allow this news to interfere with my recovery.

My recovery went quickly. I spent ten days in hospital. My young girlfriend Alisha stayed with me for the first four days, and then my chocolate boy came and looked after me. On the second week, my

girlfriend Paula came at night and slept with me.
By the end of the third week of my post-op, I asked all
my supporters to allow me to be by myself so I could
get my confidence back quickly.

> *Too much sympathy makes you weak.*
> *It fuels the flames that drives the feelings*
> *That allow the emotions to grow*
> *And destroy the spirit,*
> *Making more challenges,*
> *Which drain the energy that gives breath*
> *to life.*

Wednesday, 25th April 2017, almost five weeks after
my surgery, I woke up from the best night's sleep
since my operation. I awoke feeling perfectly whole
and complete, as if my body had never undergone
surgery, as if I had never had any pain. This same
feeling, I had fifty-two years ago waking up in Leeds
Hospital after my first valve replacement operation
and hearing all the vibrations of the universe. The
words I had been chanting and focusing on for some
days were: "I don't know." Our bodies are the most
amazing creations. The heart is God, and when we
accept and open up to this energetic power that is our
authentic selves, we can be healed.

On that fifth week post-op, I had planned to slowly
start back to work. I worked for two days on the fifth
week, doing one appointment a day. Then on the
sixth week, I did one appointment a day, working up
to two appointments a day by the eighth week, with
long rests between appointments. By week ten, I had
gone back to teaching my Monday class. During my
post-op, I made sure I went out walking every day

to the bus stop to go to the bank, the supermarket, carrying two light items, going to my hospital appointments to get my blood checks, or going to my doctor's and the pharmacy. I continued to heal and give thanks every day for health and strength. When I look back now at fourteen weeks post-op, it all seems a long time ago.

When the mind is focused on the positive,

you can heal yourself.

When the mind is focused on the negative,

you can kill yourself.

There is a message in your sickness. That's

not just for you

But that's also for the people you love. Our

experiences break and remould us.

We can either use them to live or use them to

die.

Life chooses us.
We think we make choices.
Life makes our choices, and in those choices,
we grow.
Life is a mountain; to get to the top, we have
to climb the mountain of life.
When we reach the top of our life mountain,
we see the view called experience.
Either we can use our life experiences to
become a better version of ourselves, or we
can use them to destroy ourselves and lose
out on a beautiful life.
We fall in love as it's part of our life lessons,
and the people we fall in love with are
reflections of us that teach us what we
need to learn—love, self-esteem, tolerance,
forgiveness, patience—becoming more
conscious and aware that our bodies are the
most amazing creations, and our hearts are
God. And when we accept and open up to
this energetic power that is our authentic
selves, we can find peace.

Your Heart Bible

Your heart is your Bible; it goes with you wherever you go.

It knows your future, it knows your past, it knows your truths, and it knows your lies.

You spend your time looking for love, and the love you are looking for lives inside your heart.

Your heart goes with you wherever you go.

It's there with you in all the challenges you face.

Your heart is with you in all the choices you make. The scriptures are all written in your heart.

If you talk to your heart, ask your heart what you need to know.

Your heart will open all the doors you need to walk through and close all the doors that are not for you.

Your heart never sleeps; it's the silent listener to all your conversations, responding to all your needs and walking with you on the road to your desires.

Your heart allows you to choose to feel and waits for you to ask.

Whenever you think you are alone, just listen to your heartbeat; it will remind you that you are not alone.

It answers all your questions.

Just listen to your heart when it speaks.

When you open your heart Bible and read the scripture of peace in it, you will find a passage that reads hope, joy, happiness, fulfilment, and abundance of love for your journey of discovering yourself.

Chapter 13

Who is Norma Ellis?

My life journey has taught me to become more loving, more forgiving, more attentive, more empathetic, more supportive, more understanding, more spiritual, more peaceful, and a stronger and better version of myself. I love my life.

I have learned from coming down from my physical mountaintop that there are metaphysical mountains; adversities called experiences that we have to climb. And when the experience is over for us, we must come down from the mountaintop to review life. From our mountaintops, we see other mountaintops that we would like to climb.

When we stay too long in any mountaintop experience, we run out of supplies, which are energy, water, and food, our sustenance. The mountaintop gets crowded, and it's better we come down from the mountaintop willingly instead of being pushed and breaking our spirits. It then becomes harder to prepare to climb the higher mountain we saw, when we were on top of the mountaintop, having our experience.

Nobody likes to feel hurt or rejected. When we love, we expect to be loved back in the way we are giving our love. And it's the expectations and feelings that cause the trauma in our bodies. This trauma eats away at the physical body and kills the spirit of life, causing our physical illnesses, such as my heart defect, and other illnesses some of us experience in our bodies.

We all carry secrets, deep beliefs, and fears that we are afraid to show, share, or live out. Sometimes we even have to carry secrets for other people. All our purposes lead to the same road. Emotions are the greatest feature that we all will experience, and most of us get mentally and physically damaged through our emotions.

In a relationship, loving another human being and expecting the same love in return is the most challenging thing that life has for us, whether we are conscious of it or not.

I believe in life after death and the reincarnation of our spirits in different bodies. They play life stories in reverse order for us to understand our unfinished journeys, as our bodies have a lifespan. But the consciousness of the spirit is eternal.

I believe that there is a higher power. We can agree that the higher power has a name. We can call this higher power God, Mother, Father God, Jehovah, Allah, or many other names.

My perception of this higher power is love, forgiveness, patience, joy, happiness, and peace. I believe that this higher power lives in us and through us, no matter how we show up. I believe we create our life experiences through the consciousness of our feelings.

Life is not about the things we hold in our hands; it's the things we hold in our hearts.

I have written this book from my heart and my human experiences of sixty-six years. What will be remembered most about my story is not my personal achievements that I have contributed to my culture. It won't be my relationships or my survival against all odds as the first child to survive heart valve replacement. What will be the red flag on the radar are my sexual experiences and the early age at which I discovered the pleasures and power of my body.

I can hear the conversations and discussions. They will be along the lines of, "Oh, she never had a childhood," "She was abused," "She was taken advantage of," "She was too young to understand what she was doing," "The adults should be blamed," "Who was looking after her?" "It was her environment," and, "She never had a good role model."

I was angry with my parents, and I felt that they had abandoned me. I came across my sexual power and pleasure, and when I became a young adult, it surfaced again in an uncontrollable and destructive manner. I can truly say that I understand the love and sacrifice my parents had to make and the emotions they went through to fight for me to have the opportunity to survive. I can only love them more now that I fully understand the journey and why life had to be that way. If more of us could be truthful, we would not feel so ashamed. I learned to be a survivor, and those strong survival skills came from my parents. I learned to turn all negatives into positive outcomes.

Everything that has happened in my life has happened for a purpose. There is no one to be blamed. I have no regrets about anything that I have done to make me the person I have become.

I have no sadness regarding any of my parents' parenting. They did their best with love. The skills and resources they had at that time, the way they communicated through actions and not words, and the intention of their actions were for my good. I now understand there are many ways that we can communicate love, and it's not all about hugs and kisses—which are important—but it's about survival and how we survive with each other, show and teach survival skills in the things that we do.

One thing that I have learned is that medical professionals are doing a great job, but we cannot rely only on them for our healing, as they are learning just as much as we are. When we listen to our hearts, it helps us to find solutions to our sickness.

Sometimes we have to find the strength of the child that is within us and become that child again.

I have not allowed my life experiences to kill that five-year-old child who twice survived against all odds with a heart defect. I'm still that five-year-old child in a sixty-six-year-old mind, trying to make sense of my true purpose, walking the road of life alone. The alone that I am talking about isn't about not having people in my life. This alone is a feeling that I am not truly fulfilled with all my purposes. I know that all the things I have experienced so far in my life have been preparation for some greatness that will transform not only my world, but also other people's worlds. There is a deeper passion and purpose stirring within me and a sense of knowing that there is a new mountain that I have to climb.

On a quiet Sunday, the 19th November 2017, in my deepest thoughts I asked myself, *Who is Norma? Have I truly become the best version of myself? Can I truly say that I have found the key to life?* This was my quest and the challenge I gave myself in 1990 as I departed from Florida on a Virgin Atlantic flight to return to England. As I looked down from the clouds with tears in my eyes, running away from old challenges to new challenges, I knew I had to find the key to living life and understanding my purpose in the grand scheme.

The key I found is to love myself regardless of what I have done or what has been done to me; to forgive myself and others regardless of the pain and hurt I may feel; to learn to accept myself and others, no matter how we show up; to find the good in the bad; to give love to things and to others we don't understand, and to know that change starts with me.

Peace starts with me.

Love starts with me.

Love is the key to life.

There is no greater love than that of a person who lays down his or her life for another.

It's not the body that needs to be healed, but the soul, the spirit of who we are, which has been with us over lifetimes and has repeated the same emotional responses to life's challenges over and over again. It is the soul that talks through our physical bodies. When healing touches the deeper parts of our souls and spirits, we will find peace with all there is and with all there was, as peace is who we truly are. "You are a peaceful soul."

When we truly allow peace, the body can heal, and it may be time for us to go home. Or we still may have work to complete.

Peace is allowing and accepting the outcome of our healings and our lives' destinies. Peace is joy, happiness, love.

I am a peaceful soul.

Printed in Great Britain
by Amazon